SUPERCLUBS
UNOFFICIAL
SOCCER YEARBOOK 98/99
FOR SUPPORTERS OF
DUNFERMLINE
ATHLETIC

DP
DEMPSEY
PARR

First published in Great Britain in 1998 by
Dempsey Parr
13 Whiteladies Road
Clifton
Bristol BS8 1PB

ISBN: 1840840927

Produced for Dempsey Parr by
Prima Creative Services

Editorial director Roger Kean
Managing editor Tim Smith (Content E.D.B.)
Contributing authors
Steve Bradley
Jim Drewett (Deadline Features)
Steve Farragher
Sam Johnstone
Alex Leith (Deadline Features)
Rex Nash
Russell Smith
Tim Smith

Cover background and illustrations by Oliver Frey

Design and repro by Prima Creative Services

Printed and bound in Italy by L.E.G.O., Vicenza

Picture Acknowledgements
The publisher would like to thank the staff of Allsport
and Action Images for their unstinting help and all the
other libraries, newspapers and photographers who
have made this edition possible. All pictures are
credited alongside the photograph.

PHOTO NEWS SCOTLAND

SUPERCLUBS
UNOFFICIAL
SOCCER YEARBOOK 98/99
FOR SUPPORTERS OF
DUNFERMLINE
ATHLETIC

C O N T E N T S

STATISTICS

'It's a great job, apart from Saturday afternoons,' says former Dunfermline Athletic manager Jocky Scott on the joys of sitting in the East End Park hotseat. No doubt, though, the Dunfermline managers of the 1960s would have disagreed with that downbeat statement, as The Pars enjoyed a period of great success, including two Scottish Cup triumphs. And with the club establishing itself in the Premier League again, the good times could soon be returning to Dunfermline.

Date Formed: 1885
Date Entered Football League: 1912
Former Names: None
Official Nickname: The Pars
Other Nicknames: None

MANAGERS SINCE JOINED LEAGUE:

Run by a committee	(1912–22)
William Knight	(1922–25)
Sandy Paterson	(1925–30)
William Knight	(1930–36)
David Taylor	(1936–38)
Peter Wilson	(1938–39)
Sandy Archibald	(1939–46)
William McAndrew	(1947)
Bobby Calder	(1947–48)
William Webber Lees	(1949–51)
Bobby Ansell	(1952–55)
Andy Dickson	(1955–60)
Jock Stein	(1960–64)
Willie Cunningham	(1964–67)
George Farm	(1967–70)
Alex Wright	(1970–72)
George Miller	(1972–75)
Harry Melrose	(1975–80)
Pat Stanton	(1980–82)
Tom Forsyth	(1982–83)
Jim Leishman	(1983–90)
Ian Munro	(1990–91)
Jocky Scott	(1991–93)
Bert Paton	(1993–)

'Give 'em hell!' – Bert Paton (inset) motivates the Pars to a season of achievement this term

CLUB HONOURS

First Division Champions
1989, 1996
Second Division Champions
1926, 1986
First Division Runners-Up
1987, 1994, 1995
Second Division Runners-Up
1913, 1934, 1955, 1958, 1973, 1979
Scottish Cup Winners 1961 (April 22nd, Hampden Park)
Dunfermline Athletic v Celtic 0–0
(April 26th, Hampden Park) (Replay)
Dunfermline Athletic v Celtic 2–0
Scorers: Thomson, Dickson

Scottish Cup Winners 1968 (April 27th, Hampden Park)
Dunfermline Athletic v Hearts 3–1
Scorers: Gardner (2); Lister
Scottish Cup Runners-Up 1965 (April 24th, Hampden Park)
Dunfermline Athletic v Celtic 2–3
Scorers: Melrose, McLaughlin
Scottish League Cup Runners-Up 1949
(October 29th, Hampden Park)
Dunfermline Athletic v East Fife 0–3
Scottish League (Skol) Cup Runners-Up 1991
(October 27th, Hampden Park)
Dunfermline Athletic v Hibernian 0–2

Chairman: C.R. Woodrow
Club Sponsors: Landmark Home Furnishings

PHOTO NEWS SCOTLAND

Dave Barnett makes life difficult for Celtic... again

Stadiums: 1885 – End Park
Address: East End Park, Halbeath Road,
Dunfermline, Fife KY12 7RB
Capacity: 15,925
Stands: Centre, East Wing, West Wing, North
East, North West
Prices: Adult £10–£15; Concessions £5–£9
Season ticket prices: Adult £193–£243
Concessions £88–£138
Parking facilities: North Stand car park and multi-
storey car park ten minutes walk from the ground

PITCH DIMENSIONS

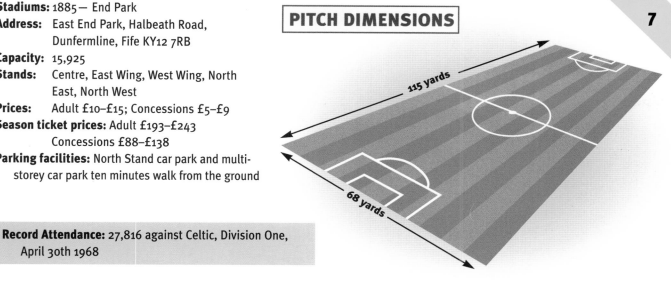

115 yards

68 yards

Record Attendance: 27,816 against Celtic, Division One,
April 30th 1968

BEST PUB

The Elizabethans, Halbeath Road (arguably the closest to the ground,
the rest are further in towards the town centre)

*While Rangers feel the
force once again too...*

PHOTO NEWS SCOTLAND

Preferred team formation: 4–4–2
Biggest rivals: St. Johnstone

Programme: The Pars Programme
Programme Editor: Duncan Simpson
Programme Price: £1.50
Bus routes to stadium: Dunfermline station
approximately 15 minutes walk from ground.

FANZINES

East End Bounce, 260 Bonnington Road, Edinburgh,
EH6 5BE

CONTACT NUMBERS

(Tel Code 01383)
● Main number 724 295
● Fax 723 468
● Ticket Office 724 295
● Matchday info 724 295
● Commercial dept 724 295
● Supporters club 611 793
● Club shop 724 295
● Clubcall 0930 555 060

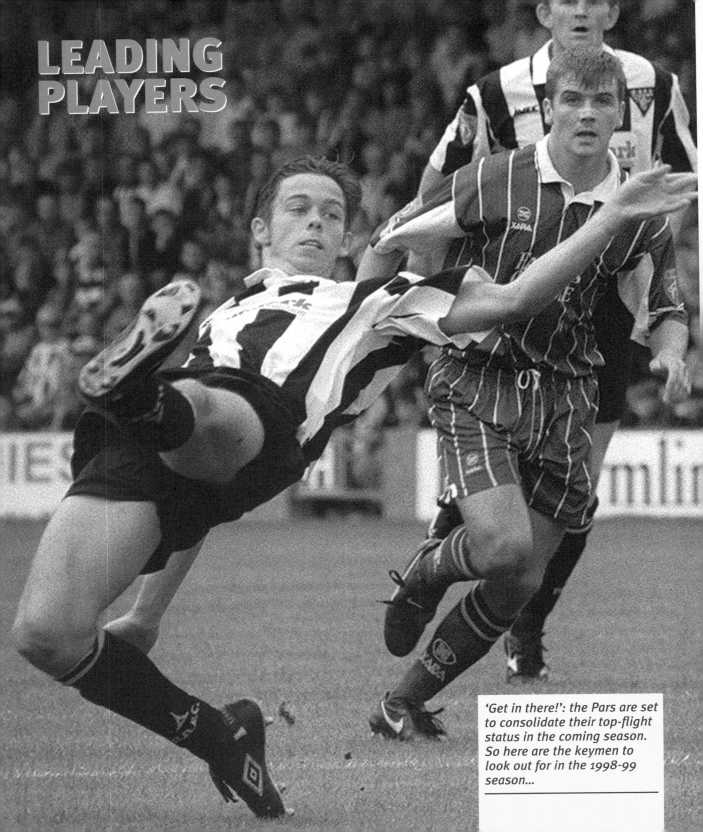

LEADING PLAYERS

'Get in there!': the Pars are set to consolidate their top-flight status in the coming season. So here are the keymen to look out for in the 1998-99 season...

1997/98 SEASON TOP 10 GOALSCORERS

Player	Goals (League/Cup)
A Smith	0 1 2 3 4 5 6 7 8 9 10 11 12 13 14 15 16 17 18 19 20 21 22 23 24 25 26 27 28 29 30 31 32 33 34 35
D Bingham	
A Tod	
H French	
G Britton	
S Petrie	
G Shaw	
M Millar	
D Barnett	
C Ireland	

LEAGUE ▇ CUP ▇

MOST LEAGUE APPEARANCES

	PLAYER	APPEARANCES	SUBSTITUTE	GOALS
1	Greg Shields	36	0	0
2	Ian Westwater	36	0	0
3	Andrew Tod	35	0	6
4	Hamish French	34	0	2
5	Andy Smith	33	0	16
6	David Bingham	17	12	5
7	Stewart Petrie	19	8	2
8	Ivo Den Bieman	10	14	0
9	Allan Moore	11	11	1
10	George Shaw	12	10	2
11	Dave Barnett	21	0	1
12	Craig Robertson	21	0	0
13	Scott McCulloch	18	0	0
14	Henry Curran	15	2	1
15	Gerard Britton	12	4	3
16	Sergio Duarte	9	7	0
17	Colin Miller	14	2	0
18	Craig Ireland	12	0	1
19	Marc Millar	9	2	2
20	Richard Huxford	9	1	0

PLAYER STATISTICS

Record transfer fee paid:
Istvan Kozma – £540,000 from Bordeaux, September 1989

Record transfer fee received:
Istvan Kozma – £300,000 from Liverpool, February 1992

Oldest player: Hamish McAlpine, 38 years and 77 days against Meadowbank Thistle, April 8th 1986

Youngest player: Alex Edwards, 16 years and 5 days against Hibernian, March 19th 1962

International captains: None

Most capped player: Istvan Kozma, 13, Hungary (1989–92)

SQUAD

IAN WESTWATER
DOB: 8/11/63
Position: Goalkeeper
Usual shirt number: 1
Joined club: March 1994 from Dundee
League Games played: 102
League Goals scored: 0
International caps: 0
League Debut: 2/3/94 v Stirling Albion (H)

DEREK FLEMING
DOB: 5/12/73
Position: Defender
Usual shirt number: 3
Joined club: October 1994 from Meadowbank Thistle
League Games played: 90
League Goals scored: 6
International caps: 0
League Debut: 8/10/94 v St Johnstone (H)

CRAIG IRELAND
DOB: 29/11/75
Position: Defender
Usual shirt number: 6
Joined club: February 1996 from Aberdeen
League Games played: 31
League Goals scored: 1
International caps: 0
League Debut: 24/2/96 v Dundee United (H)

COLIN MILLER
DOB: 4/10/64
Position: Defender
Usual shirt number: 3
Joined club: November 1995 from Heart of Midlothian
League Games played: 61
League Goals scored: 0
International caps: Canada (51)
League Debut: 4/11/95 v St Mirren (H)

PHOTO NEWS SCOTLAND

Craig Robertson's experience puts him head and shoulders above the rest

Ian Westwater's commitment to the cause provides motivation for the youngsters

RAY SHARP

DOB: 16/11/69
Position: Defender
Usual shirt number: 3
Joined club: August 1986 from Gardoch United and November 1996 from Preston North End
League Games played: 167
League Goals scored: 1
International caps: 0
League Debut: 11/3/89 against Raith Rovers (H)

GREG SHIELDS

DOB: 21/8/76
Position: Defender
Usual shirt number: 2
Joined club: June 1997 from Glasgow Rangers
League Games played: 36
League Goals scored: 0
International caps: 0
League Debut: 2/8/97 v Motherwell (H)

ANDREW TOD

DOB: 4/11/71
Position: Defender
Usual shirt number: 4
Joined club: November 1993 from Kelty Hearts
League Games played: 163
League Goals scored: 32
International caps: 0
League Debut: 4/12/93 v Morton (A)

STEVE WELSH

DOB: 19/4/68
Position: Defender
Usual shirt number: 5
Joined club: November 1996 from Peterborough United
League Games played: 26
League Goals scored: 0
International caps: 0
League Debut: 16/11/96 v Raith Rovers (A)

Old favourites combine with new faces in the coming season to ensure that the Pars' assault on a European place is well grounded

IVO DEN BIEMAN
DOB: 4/2/67
Position: Midfielder
Usual shirt number: 7
Joined club: August 1993 from Dundee
League Games played: 151
League Goals scored: 10
International caps: 0
League Debut: 7/8/93 v Falkirk (A)

SERGIO DUARTE
DOB: 20/1/66
Position: Midfielder
Usual shirt number: 8
Joined club: October 1997 from Boavista
League Games played: 16
League Goals scored: 0
International caps: 0
League Debut: 4/10/97 v Dundee United (H)

DAVID BINGHAM
DOB: 3/9/70
Position: Midfielder
Usual shirt number: 7
Joined club: September 1995 from Forfar Athletic
League Games played: 62
League Goals scored: 9
International caps: 0
League Debut: 23/9/95 v Morton (A)

PAUL McDONALD
DOB: 20/4/68
Position: Midfielder
Usual shirt number: 11
Joined club: January 1998 from Brighton
League Games played: 3
League Goals scored: 0
International caps: 0
League Debut: 10/1/98 v Hibernian (A)

HENRY CURRAN
DOB: 9/10/66
Position: Midfielder
Usual shirt number: 6
Joined club: March 1996 from Partick Thistle
League Games played: 37
League Goals scored: 2
International caps: 0
League Debut: 19/10/96 v Dundee United (H)

ALLAN MOORE
DOB: 25/12/64
Position: Midfielder
Usual shirt number: 7
Joined club: March 1994 from St Johnstone
League Games played: 96
League Goals scored: 9
International caps: 0
League Debut: 26/3/94 v Falkirk (H)

Marco Negri of Rangers looks up to Dave Barnett, who takes no prisoners. Will 1998-99 see the Auld Firm crumble under the new Pars?

PHOTO NEWS SCOTLAND

GEORGE SHAW

DOB: 10/2/69
Position: Midfielder
Usual shirt number: 7
Joined club: September 1997 from Dundee United
League Games played: 23
League Goals scored: 2
International caps: 0
League Debut: 21/9/97 v Kilmarnock (H)

GERARD BRITTON

DOB: 20/10/70
Position: Striker
Usual shirt number: 10
Joined club: July 1996 from Dundee
League Games played: 49
League Goals scored: 16
International caps: 0
League Debut: 17/8/96 v Rangers (H)

HAMISH FRENCH

DOB: 7/2/64
Position: Striker
Usual shirt number: 10
Joined club: October 1991 from Dundee United
League Games played: 81
League Goals scored: 3
International caps: 0
League Debut: 2/11/91 v St Johnstone (A)

ANDY SMITH

DOB: 27/11/68
Position: Striker
Usual shirt number: 9
Joined club: July 1995 from Airdrieonians
League Games played: 87
League Goals scored: 35
International caps: 0
League Debut: 16/12/95 v Airdrieonians (H)

STEWART PETRIE

DOB: 27/2/70
Position: Midfielder
Usual shirt number: 11
Joined club: August 1993 from Forfar Athletic
League Games played: 159
League Goals scored: 38
International caps: 0
League Debut: 28/8/93 v Airdrieonians (H)

CRAIG ROBERTSON

DOB: 22/4/63
Position: Midfielder
Usual shirt number: 8
Joined club: May 1987 from Raith Rovers and August 1991 from Aberdeen
League Games played: 277
League Goals scored: 36
International caps: 0
League Debut: 8/8/87 v Hibernian (H)

ALL-TIME RECORDS

POINTS	10	20	30	40	50	60	70	80	90	100	200	300	400	500
Aberdeen — POINTS 3448 / GOALS 5149						5		7						
Celtic — POINTS 4816 / GOALS 7336								2		2				
Dundee — POINTS 3456 / GOALS 5379									4	5				
Dundee United — POINTS 2569 / GOALS 4297										10	9			
Dunfermline Ath — POINTS 2731 / GOALS 4303										8		8		
Hearts — POINTS 3933 / GOALS 6189						3		3						
Kilmarnock — POINTS 3375 / GOALS 5291							7		6					
Motherwell — POINTS 3398 / GOALS 5631								6		4				
Rangers — POINTS 5040 / GOALS 7647										1	1			
St Johnstone — POINTS 2651 / GOALS 4255											9	10		

(9) Average position within the Premier League by points in the league since joining

(9) Average position within the Premier League by goals scored in the league since joining

	P	W	D	L	F	A	Pts			P	W	D	L	F	A	Pts
Celtic	36	22	8	6	64	24	74		Aberdeen	36	9	12	15	39	53	39
Rangers	36	21	9	6	76	38	72		Dundee United	36	8	13	15	43	51	37
Heart of Midlothian	36	18	10	7	70	46	67		Dunfermline Athletic	36	8	13	15	43	68	37
Kilmarnock	36	13	11	12	40	52	50		Motherwell	36	9	7	20	46	64	34
St Johnstone	36	13	10	13	38	42	48		Hibernian (r)	36	6	12	18	37	58	30

Dunfermline Athletic's total points since joining league **2731**

East End Park: home of Dunfermline Athletic
Aerofilms

SUPERCLUBS
UNOFFICIAL
SOCCER YEARBOOK 98/99

JULY 1998 – JUNE 1999 DIARY
AND CLUB FIXTURES

Fixture dates are subject to change.
League Cup and Scottish Cup draws were not made at press-time.

THE STORY OF SCOTTISH PREMIER LEAGUE SOCCER
IN THE 1997/98 SEASON

FOR SUPPORTERS OF
DUNFERMLINE
ATHLETIC

SCOTTISH PREMIER LEAGUE CLUB ADDRESSES

ABERDEEN
Pittodrie Stadium, Pittodrie Street, Aberdeen, AB2 1QH
Main No: 01224 650400

CELTIC
Celtic Park, 95 Kerrydale Street, Glasgow, G40 3RE
Main No: 0141 556 2611

DUNDEE
Dens Park Stadium, Sandeman Street, Dundee, DD3 7JY
Main No: 01382 826 104

DUNDEE UNITED
Tannadice Park, Tannadice Street, Dundee, DD3 7JW
Main No: 01382 833 166

DUNFERMLINE ATHLETIC
East End Park, Halbeath Road, Dunfermline, Fife, KY12 7RB
Main No: 01383 724 295

HEART OF MIDLOTHIAN
Tynecastle Park, Gorgie Road, Edinburgh, EH11 2NL
Main No: 0131 200 7200

KILMARNOCK
Rugby Park, Rugby Road, Kilmarnock, KA1 2DP
Main No: 01563 525184

MOTHERWELL
Fir Park, Motherwell, ML1 2QN
Main No: 01698 333333

RANGERS
Ibrox Stadium, Edminston Drive, Glasgow, G51 2XD
Main No: 0141 427 8500

ST JOHNSTONE
McDiarmid Park, Crieff Road, Perth, PH1 2SJ
Main No: 01738 626961

ALL-CLUB LOCATIONS

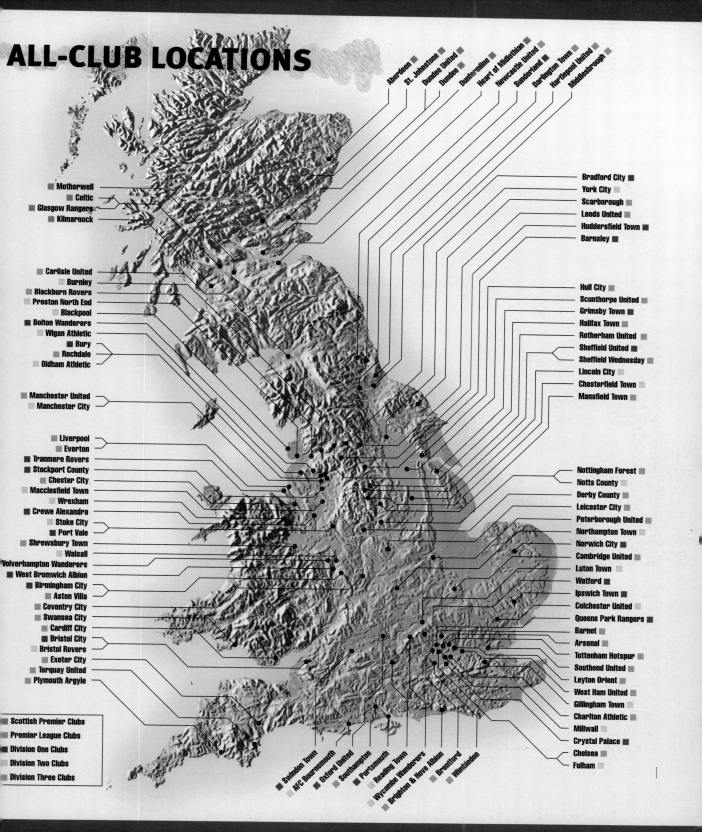

Aberdeen
St. Johnstone
Dundee United
Dundee
Dunfermline
Heart of Midlothian
Newcastle United
Sunderland
Darlington Town
Hartlepool United
Middlesbrough

Motherwell
Celtic
Glasgow Rangers
Kilmarnock

Bradford City
York City
Scarborough
Leeds United
Huddersfield Town
Barnsley

Carlisle United
Burnley
Blackburn Rovers
Preston North End
Blackpool
Bolton Wanderers
Wigan Athletic
Bury
Rochdale
Oldham Athletic

Hull City
Scunthorpe United
Grimsby Town
Halifax Town
Rotherham United
Sheffield United
Sheffield Wednesday
Lincoln City
Chesterfield Town
Mansfield Town

Manchester United
Manchester City

Liverpool
Everton
Tranmere Rovers
Stockport County
Chester City
Macclesfield Town
Wrexham
Crewe Alexandra
Stoke City
Port Vale
Shrewsbury Town
Walsall
Wolverhampton Wanderers
West Bromwich Albion
Birmingham City
Aston Villa
Coventry City
Swansea City
Cardiff City
Bristol City
Bristol Rovers
Exeter City
Torquay United
Plymouth Argyle

Nottingham Forest
Notts County
Derby County
Leicester City
Peterborough United
Northampton Town
Norwich City
Cambridge United
Luton Town
Watford
Ipswich Town
Colchester United
Queens Park Rangers
Barnet
Arsenal
Tottenham Hotspur
Southend United
Leyton Orient
West Ham United
Gillingham Town
Charlton Athletic
Millwall
Crystal Palace
Chelsea
Fulham

Swindon Town
AFC Bournemouth
Oxford United
Southampton
Portsmouth
Reading Town
Wycombe Wanderers
Brighton & Hove Albion
Brentford
Wimbledon

Scottish Premier Clubs
Premier League Clubs
Division One Clubs
Division Two Clubs
Division Three Clubs

CALENDAR 1998

January
	M	T	W	T	F	S	S
1				1	2	3	4
2	5	6	7	8	9	10	11
3	12	13	14	15	16	17	18
4	19	20	21	22	23	24	25
5	26	27	28	29	30	31	

February
	M	T	W	T	F	S	S
5							1
6	2	3	4	5	6	7	8
7	9	10	11	12	13	14	15
8	16	17	18	19	20	21	22
9	23	24	25	26	27	28	

March
	M	T	W	T	F	S	S
9							1
10	2	3	4	5	6	7	8
11	9	10	11	12	13	14	15
12	16	17	18	19	20	21	22
13	23	24	25	26	27	28	29
14	30	31					

April
	M	T	W	T	F	S	S
14		1	2	3	4	5	
15	6	7	8	9	10	11	12
16	13	14	15	16	17	18	19
17	20	21	22	23	24	25	26
18	27	28	29	30			

May
	M	T	W	T	F	S	S
18					1	2	3
19	4	5	6	7	8	9	10
20	11	12	13	14	15	16	17
21	18	19	20	21	22	23	24
22	25	26	27	28	29	30	31

June
	M	T	W	T	F	S	S
23	1	2	3	4	5	6	7
24	8	9	10	11	12	13	14
25	15	16	17	18	19	20	21
26	22	23	24	25	26	27	28
27	29	30					

July
	M	T	W	T	F	S	S
27		1	2	3	4	5	
28	6	7	8	9	10	11	12
29	13	14	15	16	17	18	19
30	20	21	22	23	24	25	26
31	27	28	29	30	31		

August
	M	T	W	T	F	S	S
31						1	2
32	3	4	5	6	7	8	9
33	10	11	12	13	14	15	16
34	17	18	19	20	21	22	23
35	24	25	26	27	28	29	30
36	31						

September
	M	T	W	T	F	S	S
36		1	2	3	4	5	6
37	7	8	9	10	11	12	13
38	14	15	16	17	18	19	20
39	21	22	23	24	25	26	27
40	28	29	30				

October
	M	T	W	T	F	S	S
40				1	2	3	4
41	5	6	7	8	9	10	11
42	12	13	14	15	16	17	18
43	19	20	21	22	23	24	25
44	26	27	28	29	30	31	

November
	M	T	W	T	F	S	S
44							1
45	2	3	4	5	6	7	8
46	9	10	11	12	13	14	15
47	16	17	18	19	20	21	22
48	23	24	25	26	27	28	29
49	30						

December
	M	T	W	T	F	S	S
49		1	2	3	4	5	6
50	7	8	9	10	11	12	13
51	14	15	16	17	18	19	20
52	21	22	23	24	25	26	27
53	28	29	30	31			

UK Holiday   Scotland Holiday   N. Ireland Holiday   Not in Scotland

CALENDAR 1999

January

	M	T	W	T	F	S	S
1					1	2	3
2	4	5	6	7	8	9	10
3	11	12	13	14	15	16	17
4	18	19	20	21	22	23	24
5	25	26	27	28	29	30	31

February

	M	T	W	T	F	S	S
6	1	2	3	4	5	6	7
7	8	9	10	11	12	13	14
8	15	16	17	18	19	20	21
9	22	23	24	25	26	27	28

March

	M	T	W	T	F	S	S
10	1	2	3	4	5	6	7
11	8	9	10	11	12	13	14
12	15	16	17	18	19	20	21
13	22	23	24	25	26	27	28
14	29	30	31				

April

	M	T	W	T	F	S	S
14				1	2	3	4
15	5	6	7	8	9	10	11
16	12	13	14	15	16	17	18
17	19	20	21	22	23	24	25
18	26	27	28	29	30		

May

	M	T	W	T	F	S	S
18						1	2
19	3	4	5	6	7	8	9
20	10	11	12	13	14	15	16
21	17	18	19	20	21	22	23
22	24	25	26	27	28	29	30
23	31						

June

	M	T	W	T	F	S	S
23		1	2	3	4	5	6
24	7	8	9	10	11	12	13
25	14	15	16	17	18	19	20
26	21	22	23	24	25	26	27
27	28	29	30				

July

	M	T	W	T	F	S	S
27				1	2	3	4
28	5	6	7	8	9	10	11
29	12	13	14	15	16	17	18
30	19	20	21	22	23	24	25
31	26	27	28	29	30	31	

August

	M	T	W	T	F	S	S
31							1
32	2	3	4	5	6	7	8
33	9	10	11	12	13	14	15
34	16	17	18	19	20	21	22
35	23	24	25	26	27	28	29
36	30	31					

September

	M	T	W	T	F	S	S
36			1	2	3	4	5
37	6	7	8	9	10	11	12
38	13	14	15	16	17	18	19
39	20	21	22	23	24	25	26
40	27	28	29	30			

October

	M	T	W	T	F	S	S
40					1	2	3
41	4	5	6	7	8	9	10
42	11	12	13	14	15	16	17
43	18	19	20	21	22	23	24
44	25	26	27	28	29	30	31

November

	M	T	W	T	F	S	S
45	1	2	3	4	5	6	7
46	8	9	10	11	12	13	14
47	15	16	17	18	19	20	21
48	22	23	24	25	26	27	28
49	29	30					

December

	M	T	W	T	F	S	S
49			1	2	3	4	5
50	6	7	8	9	10	11	12
51	13	14	15	16	17	18	19
52	20	21	22	23	24	25	26
53	27	28	29	30	31		

1998 JUNE 29 – JULY 12

Monday June 29 1998

Tuesday June 30 1998

Wednesday July 1 1998

Thursday July 2 1998

Friday July 3 1998

Saturday July 4 1998

Sunday July 5 1998

Monday July 6 1998

Tuesday July 7 1998

Wednesday July 8 1998

Thursday July 9 1998

Friday July 10 1998

Saturday July 11 1998

Sunday July 12 1998

30 July 1997: Rangers scored six goals without reply against GI Gotu of Faroe Islands in the European Champion Clubs Cup Second Qualifying round, but Dundee United went three better – it easily beat the Andorran amateurs CE Principat 9–0 on the night and 17–0 on aggregate. Gary McSwegan scored a hat trick and Robbie Winters scored two as the 'Terrors' easily passed through into the next round. CE Principat coach Manola Marin predicted Tommy McLean's men would not last long with Europe's big teams joining the tournament in the later stages. 'Dundee United may have hammered us, but they will have to play a lot better if they hope to advance against bigger clubs in the competition'.

*Celtic nerve settler:
Darren Jackson*

Celtic eased through to the next round of the UEFA cup in a good week for Scottish clubs in Europe Darren Jackson scored a goal on his home debut for Celtic at a time when the Celtic Park fans were becoming restless. They had taken the lead through Andreas Thom in the 19th minute and from then it looked as if it would be plain sailing, but the Inter Cable-Tel from the Welsh League fought hard until three minutes from the interval. After Jackson had settled the Celtic nerves, Tommy Johnson slotted home a cross and the game was effectively over. In the second half Celtic scored two more goals through Hannah and Hay and made it through to the next round 8–0 on aggregate.

*High-scoring Tannadice Park 'Terror':
Dundee United's Gary McSwegan*

Monday July 13 1998

Tuesday July 14 1998

Wednesday July 15 1998

Thursday July 16 1998

Friday July 17 1998

Saturday July 18 1998

Sunday July 19 1998

Monday July 20 1998

Tuesday July 21 1998

Wednesday July 22 1998

Thursday July 23 1998

Friday July 24 1998

Saturday July 25 1998

Sunday July 26 1998

2 August 1997: Kjell Olofsson scored the first goal of the new Premier Division season after 11 minutes. At that stage of the game it looked like United would run away with it, but St Johnstone held on and rode their luck. St Johnstone, back in the Premier Division for the first time in three years, were lucky to get a point when the former Aberdeen defender, Stewart McKimmie, put the ball past his own keeper. In fairness to McKimmie there was very little he could do after Atilla Sekeriloglu's powerful shot hit him. United lost their cool a little after the equaliser went in, but it was a big day for St Johnstone, who were pleased with the draw.

Premier Division season first scorer,
Dundee United's Kjell Olofsson

The first round of the Coca-Cola Cup started on the same day as the Premier Division. The most exciting game of the round was at Bogg Head, Dumbarton, where Queens Park were the visitors. They took the lead after 29 minutes when Scott Edgar put them ahead. It stayed that way until the 87th minute when Jamie Bruce gave Dumbarton a last gasp equaliser. That was how it stayed until the end of extra time and so the game went to penalties. Both teams had taken nine penalties each when Kevin Finlayson of Queens Park stepped up and hit the crossbar. Dumbarton had gone through 6–5. The reward for their efforts was a home tie against Aberdeen.

Warming up: Aberdeen's Mike Newell in the
pre-season friendly against Blackburn, 30/7/97

The Coca-Cola Cup second round took place a week after the first round with the Premier Division teams in the hat. The biggest scare of the round was at Fir Park where Motherwell were taken to penalties by Second Division Inverness Caledonian Thistle. The Well were two up at half-time, but Thistle battled hard and gained an equaliser through Wayne Addicote in the 87th minute, four minutes after coming off the bench. Extra time was a nervous affair with two Well players sent off and seven yellow cards shown. Nine man Motherwell hung on and then won the penalty shootout 4–1. In the other games Celtic put seven past Berwick, Aberdeen put five past Dumbarton and Raith scored the same number past Forfar.

Penalty converter:
Paul Wright of Kilmarnock

On 14 August, Paul Wright gave Kilmarnock an unlikely, but deserved victory against the Irish part-timers, Shelbourne, who had taken the league through the ex-Birmingham City player Mark Rutherford in the 12th minute. Goalkeeper Alan Gough had kept the Irish side in the lead until the 65th minute, when Kilmarnock were awarded a penalty which was converted by Wright. It was not until injury time that Wright scored his second, when he lifted the ball over Gough to send Kilmarnock into the second leg with that all important lead. Kilmarnock's game was the only highlight in a bad week in Europe for the Scottish clubs with Rangers, Celtic and Dundee United all losing away from home.

Monday July 27 1998

Tuesday July 28 1998

Wednesday July 29 1998

Thursday July 30 1998

Friday July 31 1998

Saturday August 1 1998
Dunfermline Athletic at Celtic

Sunday August 2 1998

Monday August 3 1998

Tuesday August 4 1998

Wednesday August 5 1998

Thursday August 6 1998

Friday August 7 1998

Saturday August 8 1998
League Cup 2

Sunday August 9 1998

Hibernian's Chic Charnley chases the ball against Dundee United on 17/8/97

16 August 1997: with the season four weeks old the second Premier Division games got underway with Celtic's Wim Jansen taking charge of his first home league game. His team dominated the first half, but were only one goal to the good when Andreas Thom converted a penalty after Hamish French pulled down Henrik Larsson. After the interval Dunfermline drew level when David Bingham was given time to pick his spot and slot the ball home. Then in the 77th minute a defensive error saw Malky Mackay pull down Allan Moore, and French stepped up to make amends for his earlier mistake and convert the resulting penalty. This result meant that Celtic were without a win in the Premier Division and Rangers were already in the driving seat to take their tenth championship in a row.

Who gets the ball? Dundee United's Mark Perry or Barry Lavety of Hibs?

It was Coca-Cola Cup action again this week as the cup holders Kilmarnock travelled to First Division Stirling Albion on the 20th. Craig Taggart was the architect of this unlikely victory with a brilliant display of attacking football. Stirling, who were unbeaten at this stage of the season, took the lead in the 37th minute when Taggart was brought down and Derek Anderson drove his free kick into the back of the net. From here Kilmarnock were never in the game. Taggart, who had set up four of Stirling's goals, rounded off a great night by scoring the sixth Stirling goal in the last minute. As a reward for a great display Stirling got another money spinning home tie against another struggling Premier Division side, Aberdeen.

Monday August 10 1998

Tuesday August 11 1998

Wednesday August 12 1998

Thursday August 13 1998

Friday August 14 1998

Saturday August 15 1998
Dundee at Dunfermline Athletic

Sunday August 16 1998

Monday August 17 1998

Tuesday August 18 1998

Wednesday August 19 1998
League Cup 3

Thursday August 20 1998

Friday August 21 1998

Saturday August 22 1998
Dunfermline Athletic at Motherwell

Sunday August 23 1998

16/8/97: Celtic's David Hannah is chased by Dunfermline's Allan Moore. Celtic lost 2–1...

Stealing the show:
Rangers' Marco Negri

 Marco Negri, the £3.75 million signing from Perugia, stole the show at Ibrox against Dundee. He was in blistering form as he scored five well-worked goals which took his tally to ten goals in six games. Walter Smith, the Rangers manager, was delighted with the result, thinking that United were the only team in Scotland who could threaten Rangers' hold on the Premier Division, and that Negri's solo performance might have nipped this in the bud. Paul Gascoigne, returning to the Rangers side after suspension, was also in great form until his lack of match fitness showed and he was substituted in the 71st minute. In the other games Celtic gained their first league win of the season, beating St Johnstone 2–0 away from home, and Hibernian beat Kilmarnock 4–0.

 26 August, UEFA Cup Second Qualifying round, second leg: Celtic v FC Tirol Innsbruck. What a game. Celtic looked dead and buried with seven minutes to go after the Tirol substitute Krinner hit with his first touch of the ball to make the score 4–3 on the night. At half-time the score had been 2–2 after Celtic had twice given away the lead, and now it seemed that the tie had slipped away. Yet there were still more goals to come for the Parkhead faithful. Donnelly converted a dubious penalty and Craig Burley scored in the 70th minute, taking the score to 5–4 on aggregate in Celtic's favour. Then, Krinner scored again, only for Morten Wieghorst and Burley to both score in the last two minutes to save Celtic's blushes. In the other European games Rangers drew 1–1 against IFK Gothenburg, which meant they were out of the Champions League, but moved into the UEFA cup. Dundee United drew with Trabzonspor by the same score, but lost 2–1 on aggregate, and Kilmarnock also drew 1–1 which meant they got into the next round of the Cup Winners' Cup with a 3–2 aggregate win over Shelbourne.

ALLSPORT

Big Bhoy: Celtic's Craig Burley in the epic game against FC Tirol

QUIZ 1 ABOUT DUNFERMLINE ATHLETIC

1 When did the Pars first adopt the black and white stripes?
- a) 1892
- b) 1900
- c) 1912

2 What colour shirts did they use before?
- a) Maroon
- b) All-black
- c) Red

3 How many times have the Pars played in Europe?
- a) 22
- b) 32
- c) 42

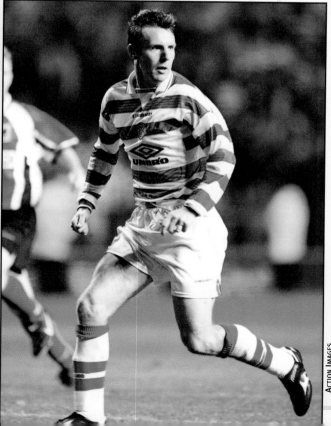

ACTION IMAGES

4 What was the aggregate score when Jock Stein's Dunfermline Athletic beat Celtic in the 1961 Scottish Cup final?
- a) 2–0
- b) 2–1
- c) 3–1

5 How many games did it take to beat Celtic?
- a) Two
- b) Three
- c) Four

6 What was the aggregate attendance?
- a) 150,000
- b) 175,000
- c) 200,000

7 How many league goals did Alex Ferguson bag in his second season at the Pars?
- a) 29
- b) 30
- c) 31

8 How much did he cost Dunfermline Athletic?
- a) No cash, he came as part of a swap deal
- b) Nothing, he was a free transfer
- c) Nothing, he was spotted by a scout

9 Which of these is NOT a Pars fanzine?
- a) 'Par Excellence'
- b) 'East End Bounce'
- c) 'Sammy Lives with Dick & Bert'

10 Which country does Par Sergio Duarte come from?
- a) Brazil
- b) Uruguay
- c) Colombia

Answers: 1.c 2.a 3.c 4.a 5.a 6.c 7.b 8.c 9.a 10.a

Monday August 24 1998

Tuesday August 25 1998

Wednesday August 26 1998

Thursday August 27 1998

Friday August 28 1998

Saturday August 29 1998
Aberdeen at Dunfermline Athletic

Sunday August 30 1998

Monday August 31 1998

Tuesday September 1 1998

Wednesday September 2 1998

Thursday September 3 1998

Friday September 4 1998

Saturday September 5 1998

Sunday September 6 1998

The last week in August was quiet for Scottish football with minds firmly fixed on the World Cup Qualifier against Belarus coming up. The games between Kilmarnock and Motherwell and the Auld Firm game at Parkhead were postponed and only three Premier League games took place. It was a very poor game in which Dundee United should have had all three points. They took the lead through Robbie Winters in the 33rd minute and that should have been that. Aberdeen scored a well-worked goal, but it was the only sparkle in their performance, and this draw meant that Aberdeen had won only three Premier Division games in the last 25.

Taking the lead:
Dundee United's Robbie Winters

30 August: In the game of the day at Dunfermline, visitors St Johnstone grabbed an unlikely point with a late equaliser after George O'Boyle had headed home in the 80th minute. Dunfermline had taken the lead after just seven minutes when Andy Tod headed home a well-directed Stewart Petrie free-kick. From then St Johnstone were playing catch up. Dunfermline were unlucky not to go into the half-time break four goals up after they hit the woodwork on three occasions. In the second half, Saints came more into the match and scored an equaliser on 68 minutes, but nine minutes later Tod scored his second to make it 2–1 to Dunfermline.

Going for the ball: Rangers' Stale Stensaas and Stephan Petterson of Gothenburg on 27/8/97

Monday September 7 1998

Tuesday September 8 1998

Wednesday September 9 1998
League Cup 4

Thursday September 10 1998

Friday September 11 1998

Saturday September 12 1998
Dunfermline Athletic at St Johnstone

Sunday September 13 1998

Monday September 14 1998

Tuesday September 15 1998

Wednesday September 16 1998

Thursday September 17 1998

Friday September 18 1998

Saturday September 19 1998
Heart of Midlothian at Dunfermline Athletic

Sunday September 20 1998

7 September: Scotland took a huge step towards qualification for France 98 after a thoroughly professional display against Belarus. This was in stark contrast to the farce played out during the week. Following the burial of Diana, Princess of Wales, Craig Brown was concerned that the public grief, and the confusion over whether the game would be played, would affect his squad. All thoughts of sadness were wiped from Scottish minds when Kevin Gallagher popped up to score an easy goal after the keeper had spilled the ball in just the sixth minute. From here it was plain sailing for the Scots, although they had to wait until the 54th minute when David Hopkin on as a substitute, scored the second. Gallagher scored his own second four minutes later and Hopkin rounded things off with his second with a great strike.

Scoring substitute: Scotland's David Hopkin celebrates one of his goals

At Ibrox, two days later, Garry McSwegan of Dundee United scored with a blinding volley in the shock of the round as they went on to beat Rangers 1–0 after extra time. Rangers had controlled most of the game and had only themselves to blame when they did not run out easy winners. They missed a host of chances, the worst coming from Marco Negri who had scored five goals in the corresponding league fixture earlier in the season. United's only chance of the game came in the 96th minute when McSwegan produced his flash of inspiration. Rangers should have won the match and would rue the chances that they did not put away. United now faced Aberdeen in the semi-final.

Dragged to a draw: Tony Vidma of Rangers in the 3–3 draw against Aberdeen on 14/9/97

Monday September 21 1998

Tuesday September 22 1998
Dunfermline Athletic at Dundee United

Wednesday September 23 1998

Thursday September 24 1998

Friday September 25 1998

Saturday September 26 1998
Rangers at Dunfermline Athletic

Sunday September 27 1998

Monday September 28 1998

Tuesday September 29 1998

Wednesday September 30 1998

Thursday October 1 1998

Friday October 2 1998

Saturday October 3 1998
Dunfermline Athletic at Kilmarnock

Sunday October 4 1998

Five days later, back in Europe in the UEFA cup, Celtic were pitted against Liverpool in a game nicknamed 'The Battle of Britain'. Celtic had battled well to take the lead, but a brilliant last-minute solo effort from Liverpool's Steve McManaman made the score 2–2. McManaman picked the ball up in his own half and ran 40 yards before unleashing an unstoppable shot into the bottom corner. The young Michael Owen had put Liverpool ahead after just 5 minutes, but Celtic didn't let their heads drop and fought hard. Spurred on by the crowd, Celtic suddenly came to life and in the 53rd minute Jackie McNamara struck a fearsome shot to the top corner that left David James in the Liverpool goal motionless. From here Celtic were on a roll and they got a deserved goal through a Simon Donnelly penalty in the 74th minute, but a moment of McManaman magic ensured that Celtic had a lot of hard work in the second leg at Anfield.

Floored: Celtic's Stephane Mahe is vaulted by Liverpool's Karl-Heinz Riedle

16 September: Jorg Albertz gave Rangers a chance of progressing through to the next round of the UEFA cup after they lost 2–1 to RC Strasbourg away from home. Rangers were unlucky not to have gained a draw when Charlie Miller failed to hit the target in the dying minutes after he was given space in the box to shoot. It was an open, clean contest, but it was three penalties that settled the game. Gerald Baticle, the Strasbourg midfielder, was bundled over for the first penalty, which he scored. Now Albertz scored his penalty for Rangers, but Baticle again was fouled in the area, and scored from the spot.

Hard work: Stephane Mahe is chased by brilliant Steve McManaman of Liverpool

Monday October 5 1998

Tuesday October 6 1998

Wednesday October 7 1998

Thursday October 8 1998

Friday October 9 1998

Saturday October 10 1998

Sunday October 11 1998

Monday October 12 1998

Tuesday October 13 1998

Wednesday October 14 1998

Thursday October 15 1998

Friday October 16 1998

Saturday October 17 1998
Celtic at Dunfermline Athletic

Sunday October 18 1998

 Celtic managed to keep the pressure on Rangers at the top of the league after their comfortable 2–0 win over bottom-of-the-table Aberdeen on 20 September. Celtic had to thank Henrik Larsson for his two first-half goals, one a well taken turn and shot past Jim Leighton, the other a great curling free-kick. Aberdeen manager Roy Aitken must have been glad that Celtic's mid-week European clash with Liverpool had taken its toll and they took their foot off the accelerator after scoring twice. The pressure on him was mounting and this defeat did nothing to stop fears that he would soon be sacked from Pittodrie.

Man to thank:
Celtic's Henrik Larsson

 Paul Lambert was in the news again that week. His German club, Borussia Dortmund, the previous season's Champions League winners, and Celtic were in talks to bring the Scottish International back home. Lambert, although enjoying life on the Continent, wanted to come back because his wife and children were finding it difficult to settle in Germany. Dortmund said that they wanted the player to stay with them and would do their utmost to help Lambert's family to settle. Since joining Dortmund, Lambert became a regular for both club and country. This was in total contrast to the end of the 1996-97 season when not one offer was made for him when his contract with Motherwell expired. Dortmund had promised to do all they could to help them settle and would review the situation at the end of the season.

*Happier back home from the Continent:
Celtic's Paul Lambert*

30 September: Rangers crashed out of the UEFA cup against RC Strasbourg after a disastrous 2–1 defeat at home. They had done all the hard work in the away leg by getting the all important away goal and then threw it away. They started well enough when Rino Gattuso scored after just 12 minutes, but Strasbourg scored either side of half-time and the game was over. Strasbourg's Kinet was sent off after 59 minutes, but by then the tie was out of reach of Rangers. Strasbourg, who were second from the bottom of the French League, were technically superior to Rangers, and this game showed how far behind the leagues of Europe Scottish football is.

Worrying odds: Rangers manager Walter Smith ponders Europe

All the talk of the first week in October was about the up-and-coming World Cup Qualifier against Latvia. The majority of the talk concerned St Johnstone keeper Alan Main who profited from Andy Goram's misfortune when he was called up to the Scotland squad for the first time, as Goram withdrew from the squad for this important game due to a knee injury. He had been pushing for a recall after losing the number one jersey to Aberdeen's Jim Leighton, but the injury news meant that Leighton would stay in goal. There were other injury worries too, with Ally McCoist and Billy McKinley struggling with hamstring and ankle problems respectively.

Injury worries: St Johnstone's Andy Goram reaches for the ball against Celtic

ACTION IMAGES

QUIZ 2 REFEREE QUIZ

1 In the event of the crossbar being broken, or somehow moved from its position, and replacing it is not possible, the referee will:
- a) Allow another item such as a taut rope to be used as a replacement.
- b) Allow play to continue without a crossbar
- c) Abandon the game.

2 The minimum height for a corner flagpole is
- a) 1.5m
- b) 5m
- c) 1.75m

3 A goal is scored from a throw-in. Does the referee:
- a) Disallow it?
- b) Use his discretion?
- c) Allow the goal?

4 Only eight players appear for one side in a professional eleven-a-side game. Does the referee:
- a) Abandon the game?
- b) Allow the game to continue?
- c) Allow non-registered players to fill-in and continue the game?

5 An outfield player swaps positions with the goalkeeper without informing the referee. The ref notices while the ball is in play. Does he?
- a) Immediately send both players off?
- b) Allow play to continue and wait for a natural break?
- c) Immediately book both players?

6 The ref gives a direct free kick in your penalty area. One of your players kicks it back to the keeper who misses the ball completely. The ball goes into your own net! Does the referee:
- a) Order the free kick to be taken again?
- b) Award a goal to the opposition?
- c) Award a corner-kick to the opposition?

7 What is wrong with the picture at the top of a penalty shoot-out?
- a) The goalkeeper of the team taking the kick is in the centre circle with the rest of his teammates. Should he be standing on the 18-yard line?
- b) The goalkeeper has his arms raised when they should be still and by his side?
- c) The referee is in the penalty area causing a distraction when he should be standing on the 18-yard line.

8 There are three minutes left in a game when one manager decides to make a substitution. Two minutes later the ball goes out of play, it takes one minute to make the substitution. Does the referee:
- a) Blow the whistle for full-time when the player enters the field?
- b) Book the manager for time-wasting?
- c) Add time on for the substitution?

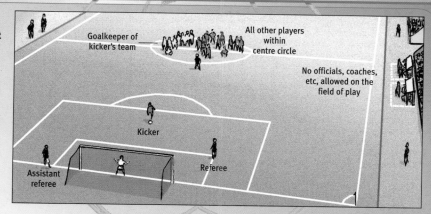

Goalkeeper of kicker's team

All other players within centre circle

No officials, coaches, etc, allowed on the field of play

Kicker

Assistant referee

Referee

9 What is wrong with this picture of the 'Technical Area'?

- a) Nothing.
- b) There are no markings showing the correct distance.
- c) The distances shown are wrong.

10 In this picture, does the referee:
- a) Give the goal?
- b) Not give the goal?
- c) Give a drop-ball?

Monday October 19 1998

Tuesday October 20 1998

Wednesday October 21 1998

Thursday October 22 1998

Friday October 23 1998

Saturday October 24 1998
Dunfermline Athletic at Dundee

Sunday October 25 1998
League Cup semi-finals

Monday October 26 1998

Tuesday October 27 1998

Wednesday October 28 1998

Thursday October 29 1998

Friday October 30 1998

Saturday October 31 1998
St Johnstone at Dunfermline Athletic

Sunday November 1 1998

Scotland's World Cup qualifier against Latvia on 11 October meant there were no Premier Division games, but what a night for Scottish football. The internationals took the field needing a win against Latvia and Spain to beat the Faeroe Islands. It was a tense affair right until the final 10 minutes. Scotland took the lead on 43 minutes when Blackburn's Kevin Gallagher scored a close range header after the Latvian goalkeeper had only parried a John Collins long range shot. Scotland pressed for a second, but it was not until the 80th minute when Man of the Match, Gordon Durie, headed the ball home. Gallagher hit the crossbar with a clever chip, but Durie who had run all night was there to follow it up. A great night for Scotland as they made it to their sixth World Cup in the last seven attempts.

Scoring for Celtic:
Craig Burley

It was Coca-Cola Cup semi-final week, with Aberdeen against Dundee United, and Celtic playing Dunfermline. Dundee United ran out comfortable 3–1 winners against the Dons thanks to two spectacular goals by Robbie Winters, which increased the pressure on Dons manager Roy Aitken. In the other game Celtic managed their first win in nine visits to Ibrox including their Cup defeats by Raith and Falkirk. Their 1–0 victory was thanks to a Craig Burley goal in the 70th minute although Dunfermline had played solidly without ever really threatening the Celtic goal. The wet, muddy conditions did not help flowing football on a night when wellington boots were needed.

Strong for Rangers, brave for Scotland:
Gordon Durie never flags

Monday November 2 1998

Tuesday November 3 1998

Wednesday November 4 1998

Thursday November 5 1998

Friday November 6 1998

Saturday November 7 1998
Dunfermline Athletic at Aberdeen

Sunday November 8 1998

Monday November 9 1998

Tuesday November 10 1998

Wednesday November 11 1998

Thursday November 12 1998

Friday November 13 1998

Saturday November 14 1998

Sunday November 15 1998
Dundee Utd at Dunfermline Athletic

Paul Gascoigne scored two goals and received the Man of the Match award for his performance against Dunfermline Athletic on 18 October. During that week, there was a great deal of speculation about Gazza's Ibrox future, with a number of reports suggesting he was to move back to England. Not for the first time in the season Gascoigne's performance was overshadowed by Marco Negri who scored another four goals to take his tally for the season to 22. Rangers went to the top of the Scottish Premier Division table for the first time this season and were the only unbeaten side in the division.

Morten Wieghorst of Celtic

Also that week, the Scottish League had a meeting to decide the future of Scottish Football. The 10 Premier Division teams were keen to speed up the process that would allow them to retire from the League. The top flight sides wanted a new league set up for next season, but their efforts were stalled by determined lower division opposition. At the last League management committee's meeting only four of the 10 breakaway clubs' motions to retire from the league were passed – Dunfermline, Hearts, Motherwell and Kilmarnock. The remaining six Premier Division clubs, including the Auld Firm, lost out as they each had members on the 12-man committee who were denied the chance to vote on their own side's motion. Premier Division spokesman Lex Gold indicated that the decision was farcical and pledged to press forward and resolve the issue.

*Mixed blessing: erratic Paul Gascoigne was
soon to leave Rangers for Middlesbrough...*

Monday November 16 1998

Tuesday November 17 1998

Wednesday November 18 1998

Thursday November 19 1998

Friday November 20 1998

Saturday November 21 1998
Dunfermline Athletic at Heart of Midlothian

Sunday November 22 1998

Monday November 23 1998

Tuesday November 24 1998

Wednesday November 25 1998

Thursday November 26 1998

Friday November 27 1998

Saturday November 28 1998
Kilmarnock at Dunfermline Athletic

Sunday November 29 1998
League Cup Final

On 25 October, Marco Negri hit the back of the net for the 23rd time that season making it nine games in a row in which he scored, breaking Hibs midfielder Ally MacLeod's 1977-78 season record. Yet he was a disappointed man after Rangers' third game of the season against Dundee United. Andy Goram failed to make an easy clearance and was tackled by Robbie Winters who put the ball in the empty net. Negri pulled one back, but Steve Pressley scored a penalty for United to seal a famous victory. Rangers' misery was compounded when Celtic won 2–0 against St Johnstone to leapfrog them and go top of the Premier Division.

At loggerheads: Dundee's Sieb Dykshra and Rangers' Marco Negri

That same week, Walter Smith, the Rangers manager, announced he would resign at the end of the season. There were a number of reasons for Smith wanting to leave. The most obvious of these was Rangers' upset in Europe. Their lack of success there had been a thorn in the side of the management for a number of seasons, and the home and away defeat at the hands of Strasbourg in the UEFA cup was the last straw. Smith also cited the lack of competition in the Premier Division. He said the only thing that kept him going that season was the thought of the unprecedented ten-in-a-row. Since Smith took over in 1991, Rangers had won thirteen domestic trophies, including seven league championships, and had reached the semi-final of the European cup back 1992-93.

Bad day for Rangers: Gers' Gascoigne is shadowed by United's Craig Easton, 25/10/97

Monday November 30 1998

Tuesday December 1 1998

Wednesday December 2 1998

Thursday December 3 1998

Friday December 4 1998

Saturday December 5 1998
Dunfermline Athletic at Rangers

Sunday December 6 1998

Monday December 7 1998

Tuesday December 8 1998

Wednesday December 9 1998

Thursday December 10 1998

Friday December 11 1998

Saturday December 12 1998
Motherwell at Dunfermline Athletic

Sunday December 13 1998

On 1 November, Marco Negri became the most prolific scorer in Scottish football when he scored in his 10th successive League game (against Kilmarnock) to beat Andy Cunningham's mark of nine, established 70 years ago. He scored his first on five minutes, but had to wait until the last three minutes to score his second and third. The first was a well-worked training ground free-kick, headed home with ease. Kilmarnock equalised on 43 minutes through Ally Mitchell who reacted first to a loose ball in the Rangers box. The game turned on 77 minutes when Kevin McGowne was sent off for a cynical challenge on Rino Gattuso. Up to this point Kilmarnock had been holding Rangers by means both fair and foul and looked as though they were capable of getting a point, until, of course, up stepped the redoubtable Negri.

Record buster: Marco Negri just scored and scored...

This week saw Paul Lambert's return home to Scotland, joining Celtic for £1.7 million from Borussia Dortmund, where he had won a European Cup winners' medal. He'd moved to Dortmund from Motherwell under the Bosman ruling after they had played each other in the UEFA cup. A strong performance convinced then Dortmund coach Ottmar Hitzfeld to sign the Scottish International. He moved into Patrik Berger's house after Berger joined Liverpool and became popular with German players and supporters, but his wife found it difficult to settle. Lambert made his debut against Rangers in the first Auld Firm derby of the season at Ibrox.

Scottish international, Paul Lambert, makes life difficult for Rangers' Jorg Albertz

ALLSPOR

Old Firm derby: Rino Gattuso leaves Celtic's Tom Boyd behind in the match that ended 1–0 for Rangers

Over recent seasons it had been the four Auld Firm derbies that settled the destination of the Scottish Premier Division title and this season looked as though it would be no different. On 11 November, a crowd of over 50,000 roared Rangers on and helped them overcome local rivals Celtic. Rangers finally looked to have gelled as a team; something they hadn't managed to do so far even though they were winning. This was the first league game of the season that Marco Negri didn't score in, but he played an influential role. His reputation had gone before him and the Celtic defence spent too much time concentrating on him, leaving space for others to cause the damage. The game was won from the unlikely source of Richard Gough on 28 minutes, and Rangers were disappointed not to have scored more goals in a game they controlled with ease. In the day's other derby in Edinburgh, Hearts beat Hibs by two goals to nil.

It was a bad week for Aberdeen. On Sunday their striker Dean Windass was sent off three times in a game against Dundee United. He was sent off for two bookable offences, the first of which he received for a terrible tackle in just 12 seconds. He was sent off in the first half after United had scored the third goal in the 21st minute. He was then shown the red card for back chat and received a third red card for ripping up a corner flag as he walked off the field. The result condemned the Aberdeen manager, Roy Aitken, and he wa sacked the following day. Aitken was the first Premier Division manager to lose his job. Ex-Spurs manager Keith Burkinshaw took ove as the caretaker manager.

QUIZ 3 ABOUT DUNFERMLINE ATHLETIC

1 **What happened in March 1998 on Bert Paton's first game back following his suspension?**
a) He was suspended again
b) His assistant Dick Campbell was 'sent-off' to the stands
c) Paton was booked but not 'sent-off'

2 **Where was Dave Barnett loaned to in 1998?**
a) Port Vale
b) Stoke City
c) Raith Rovers

3 **Who did Dunfermline Athletic beat to make certain of Premiership football for 1998-99?**
a) St Johnstone
b) Rangers
c) Motherwell

4 **Who scored the goals that confirmed the place?**
a) Andy Smith
b) Dave Barnett
c) Harry Curran

5 **Where does Symon Kaldyob, who trialled with Dunfermline Athletic come from?**
a) Nigeria
b) Cameroon
c) England

6 **How many bookings did Marc Millar pick up against Aberdeen in the same game in 1997?**
a) Three
b) Two
c) One

7 **Which of the following is NOT a reason given for the 'Pars' nickname?**
a) Named after the Plymouth Argyle (Rosyth) Supporters' Club
b) Named because the team strip featured parallel lines
c) Named because two games were Pardoned for affray during a famous 1909 game

8 **Who were Dunfermline Athletic's most recent European opposition?**
a) Anderlecht
b) Real Betis
c) Ajax

9 **Who did the Pars beat in the quarter-finals of the 1968-69 European Cup Winners' Cup?**
a) Liverpool
b) Manchester United
c) West Bromwich Albion

10 **How many times did Norrie McCathie play for Dunfermline Athletic?**
a) 560
b) 561
c) 562

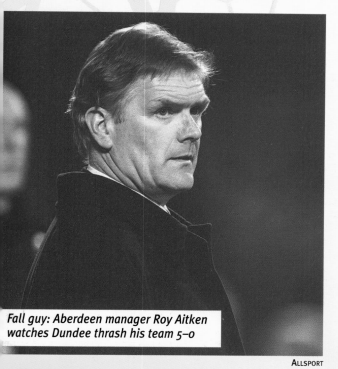

Fall guy: Aberdeen manager Roy Aitken watches Dundee thrash his team 5–0

ALLSPORT

Answers: 1.b 2.a 3.c 4.a 5.b 6.a 7.c 8.a 9.c 10.b

Monday December 14 1998

Tuesday December 15 1998

Wednesday December 16 1998

Thursday December 17 1998

Friday December 18 1998

Saturday December 19 1998
Dunfermline Athletic at Celtic

Sunday December 20 1998

Monday December 21 1998

Tuesday December 22 1998

Wednesday December 23 1998

Thursday December 24 1998

Friday December 25 1998

Saturday December 26 1998
Aberdeen at Dunfermline Athletic

Sunday December 27 1998

The second Auld Firm derby of the season took place on Wednesday 19 November. And what a night it was to turn out to be. Alan Stubbs grabbed Celtic's equaliser late in injury time in one of the most memorable Celtic v Rangers games for some years. Stubbs headed home a Jackie McNamara cross to keep Celtic in the title race, but the draw stretched Rangers' unbeaten run to 10 league games. They had taken the lead on 71 minutes through Marco Negri, his 27th goal of the season. Gordon Durie, who had an outstanding game, provided the pass. Yet it was Gascoigne again making the headlines. He was sent off after 58 minutes. Whilst in possession, Gascoigne seemed to be unfairly halted by Morten Wieghorst, and turned and swiped at his face. The stand-in referee, John Rowbotham, had no alternative but to send him off.

18/11/97: David Rowson of Dundee holds Aberdeen's Erik Pederson

Later that week, Paul Gascoigne was given a five match ban by the Scottish FA. Gascoigne already had nine disciplinary points and his sending off took him to 21, ensuring an automatic ban. Morten Wieghorst, victim of Gascoigne's aggression, went to his defence saying he pulled Gazza's shirt and the TV pictures showed that there was minimal contact. Wieghorst believed the punishment was too severe. This was the England midfielder's first red card in the Scottish Premier Division. Gascoigne missed all Rangers matches in December including the game against this week's league leaders, Hearts. He finally returned on January 1st when Rangers ironically played Celtic.

Keeping the ball: Celtic's Jackie McNamara does some nifty footwork

Monday December 28 1998

Tuesday December 29 1998
Dunfermline Athletic at St Johnstone

Wednesday December 30 1998

Thursday December 31 1998

Friday January 1 1999

Saturday January 2 1999   Sunday January 3 1999
Heart of Midlothian at Dunfermline Athletic

Monday January 4 1999

Tuesday January 5 1999

Wednesday January 6 1999

Thursday January 7 1999

Friday January 8 1999

Saturday January 9 1999   Sunday January 10 1999

End of November, the Premier Division's aim of a new 'Super League' took another twist as the Chairman of the Scottish Football League, Doug Brown, used his casting vote against the ten 'breakaway' clubs after the initial vote was tied 6–6. The 30 smaller clubs looked like they would get the written financial guarantees that would safeguard their stability, a condition they wanted met before backing any breakaway from the SFA. An agreement seemed possible to put the new league in place before August 1998, in time for the new season. Hibernian chairman Lex Gold, spokesman for the breakaway group, said: 'The result is disappointing but it will not deflect the Premier Division clubs.'

30/11/97: cheers from Blinker for Henrik Larsson's 2nd goal for Celtic

Paul Hegarty became the assistant coach to Alex Miller at Aberdeen that week after a successful time in management with both Hearts and Scotland. In the 1996-97 season Hegarty won the Premier Division reserve team title with Hearts and did well with the Scotland Under-17 side under Craig Brown. These achievements impressed the Board at Aberdeen and led to his appointment. He was seen as a man who could bring on the young players and help Miller rejuvenate the Pittodrie side. There had been some big changes at Aberdeen since Miller had taken over from Roy Aitken, such as the appointment of Hegarty and the arrival of Keith Burkinshaw as the Director of Football who would also oversee the youth development programme.

Coca Cola Cup Final: Dundee's Magnus Skoldmark intercepts Regi Blinker of Celtic

Monday January 11 1999

Tuesday January 12 1999

Wednesday January 13 1999

Thursday January 14 1999

Friday January 15 1999

Saturday January 16 1999

Sunday January 17 1999

Monday January 18 1999

Tuesday January 19 1999

Wednesday January 20 1999

Thursday January 21 1999

Friday January 22 1999

Saturday January 23 1999
Scottish Cup 3

Sunday January 24 1999

In a one-sided Coca-Cola Cup Final on 30 November, Celtic overcame Dundee United to win the trophy for the first time in 15 years. The men from Tannadice effectively lost the game in the first 20 minutes when they seemed to freeze as the nerves of the occasion got to them. By the time they came into the game Celtic were two goals up and in complete control. Superior tactics created the first goal: The Man of the Match, Celtic midfielder Morten Wieghorst, gave the ball to Andreas Thom who delivered a cross for Mark Rieper to head home. The celebrations continued just three minutes later when Henrik Larson struck a powerful shot from 20 yards which went in after a deflection off Maurice Malpass. United came back in the second half, but by then it was all over and the game was finally wrapped up in the 59th minute when Burley headed home after brilliant work from Regi Blinker. Finally.

Maurice Malpass
of Dundee United in action

After a reasonable season so far St Johnstone were looking to strengthen their squad. Having made a breakthrough in getting the Swedish striker Lars Gunner Karlstrand to agree to a move to the Perth club, they hit a snag. The problem arose in connection with Britain's strict quarantine laws. Karlstrand was keen to see that his Rottweiler, Ted, spent as little time in quarantine as possible. The Swede then decided he would have to think again about the transfer saying 'Ted's very precious to me. Hopefully I can get something sorted out.' Karlstrand then stalled the deal that eventually never came off.

Will 1998/99 be the season that sees George O'Boyle find the quality all are sure is there?

Monday January 25 1999

Tuesday January 26 1999

Wednesday January 27 1999

Thursday January 28 1999

Friday January 29 1999

Saturday January 30 1999
Dunfermline Athletic at Dundee United

Sunday January 31 1999

Monday February 1 1999

Tuesday February 2 1999

Wednesday February 3 1999

Thursday February 4 1999

Friday February 5 1999

Saturday February 6 1999
Rangers at Dunfermline Athletic

Sunday February 7 1999

The future of the breakaway by the top 10 clubs from the Scottish Football League took a strange turn on 11 December. Chris Robinson, the chairman of Hearts Football Club announced that the 10 Premier Division chairmen had agreed a plan to do away with promotion or relegation to the top flight at the end of the season. The news stunned Dundee, who were at the top of the table at the time and so would have been automatically promoted to the current Premier Division. This latest development came from the 10 rebel clubs who believed they had not received sufficient help and support from the First Division clubs. In reply the rebel teams were told they could be taken to court and a ban from European competition could be involved.

Getting out of Division One will need total commitment from the Hibbies

Darren Jackson was Celtic's hero when he scored his first goal on 9 December after a three month lay-off following brain surgery. In a match Celtic had to win to keep their Championship dreams alive, manager Wim Jansen took a chance on Jackson. In the 71st minute he seized his chance to score after Regi Blinker's shot had only been parried by Aberdeen goalkeeper Jim Leighton. Jackson's goal doubled Celtic's lead after Henrik Larsen put them one up in the first half. For Jackson this was a special day, not only his first start, but a very well-taken goal. The win kept Celtic in the hunt after they had taken just two points from their last four games.

*Recovered: Celtic's Darren Jackson made a
winning return at the end of the year*

PHOTO NEWS SCOTLAND

Dunfermline's Andrew Smith and Sergio Porrini fight for the ball in the Pars 0–7 drubbing by the Bears

15 December, and a host of injuries and suspensions to Rangers almost saw the 'Fifers' (Dunfermline) pull off an unlikely victory. Instead they settled for the draw. The two dropped points meant that Rangers failed to regain top spot in the Premier League, leaving Hearts with a one point lead. The best chance of the game fell to Dunfermline in the fourth minute when a brilliant pass from Dave Bingham put through Andy Tod. It showed the inadequacies of the Rangers defence, but Tod should have tested reserve goalkeeper Thoe Snelders from six yards out. Rangers' Italian player, Rino Gattuso, picking up a clever back heel from his impressive national compatriot, Marco Negri, missed the simplest of chances when it should have been easy to score.

Alex Miller and his Aberdeen management team had a busy week. After spending time looking at two youngsters, Stevie Searle and Sam Stockley from Barnet in the English Second Division, they bought former Celtic central defender, Derek Whyte, from Middlesbrough. This was Alex Miller's first signing for the Dons since taking over as the manager earlier in the season. Aberdeen sent new Director of Football, Keith Burkenshaw, to view the Barnet players and both were seen as promising targets for the new manager, but it was the 29 year-old Whyte who made the move back to the north, for an undisclosed fee.

Quiz 4 About Scottish Premier League

1 When did Celtic last win the Premier Division?
a) 1986
b) 1987
c) 1988

2 Who was Scottish Player of the Year in 1996?
a) Paul Gascoigne
b) Ally McCoist
c) Brian Laudrup

3 How many clubs have won the Premier Division title?
a) Three
b) Four
c) Five

4 Who won the first-ever Premier Division title?
a) Rangers
b) Celtic
c) Dundee United

5 Who scored five times against Morton in a Premier Division match in 1984?
a) Mo Johnston
b) Davie Cooper
c) Paul Sturrock

6 Who was the Premier Division's top scorer in the 1983-84 season?
a) Willie Miller
b) Brian McClair
c) Charlie Nicholas

7 Who won the Premier Division title in 1983?
a) Aberdeen
b) Celtic
c) Dundee United

8 How many goals did Rangers concede in 36 Premiership matches in 1990?
a) 13
b) 19
c) 23

9 When was the last time the Premier Division was won by a club not from Glasgow?
a) 1983
b) 1984
c) 1985

10 Who was top scorer in the first-ever Premier Division season?
a) Derek Johnstone
b) Kenny Dalglish
c) Andy Gray

Looking for talent: Aberdeen manager Alex Miller

ALLSPORT

Answers: 1.c 2.a 3.b 4.a 5.c 6.b 7.c 8.b 9.c 10.b

Monday February 8 1999

Tuesday February 9 1999

Wednesday February 10 1999

Thursday February 11 1999

Friday February 12 1999

Saturday February 13 1999
Scottish Cup 4

Sunday February 14 1999

Monday February 15 1999

Tuesday February 16 1999

Wednesday February 17 1999

Thursday February 18 1999

Friday February 19 1999

Saturday February 20 1999
Dunfermline Athletic at Kilmarnock

Sunday February 21 1999

20 December: facing their most important game of the season so far, Rangers showed the sort of skill and style they needed to complete a 10th winning championship season. The victory took Rangers to the top of the league, leapfrogging over Hearts. Initially it looked as though it could have been close with Rangers missing Andy Goram, Richard Gough, Paul Gascoigne and Jonas Thern, but Gordon Durie and Jorg Albertz made the difference. Durie gave Rangers the lead on six minutes, and from there they never looked back. It was an ominous sign of what was to come for Hearts. All the Rangers side gave a great performance; even the sending off of Rino Gattuso in the 70th minute made no difference to their dominance. Durie scored his third in the 86th minute after he latched onto a pass from Laudrup to score the best goal of the night.

Hat-trick: Rangers' Gordon Durie scores his 3rd goal against Hearts

If Rangers could do it so could Celtic. Their 5–0 drubbing of Hibs that same day was one of their most impressive displays of the season. Celtic's best players were the Dutch masters Henrik Larsson and Regi Blinker, who swept all before them. The deadlock was broken on 23 minutes when Craig Burley powered home a Jackie McNamara pass after brilliant build-up work. Larsson was booked for over-celebrating. Five minutes before half-time Morten Wieghorst jumped above the static Hibs defence to head home one of his easiest goals this season. The pain became worse for Hibs in the second half with both McNamara and Larsson scoring in the second half before Burley scored the goal of the game on the stroke of full time. McNamara pushed a short corner to Burley and from 25 yards out he smashed the ball home.

63

No contest: Ian Ferguson of Rangers battles Hearts' Colin Cameron

Monday February 22 1999

Tuesday February 23 1999

Wednesday February 24 1999

Thursday February 25 1999

Friday February 26 1999

Saturday February 27 1999
Dunfermline Athletic at Motherwell

Sunday February 28 1999

Monday March 1 1999

Tuesday March 2 1999

Wednesday March 3 1999

Thursday March 4 1999

Friday March 5 1999

Saturday March 6 1999
Scottish Cup 5

Sunday March 7 1999

1 January 1998: After taking what looked to be an unassailable lead at Tynecastle, Hearts threw it and their title chances away by failing in what should have been an easy game. Kevin Harper of Hibernian put in a terrific second half display that showed the fight that the Easter Road team was capable of. It was Jim Duffy's first point from the Edinburgh derby in five attempts, but still left Hibs without a win in 15 games. Steve Fulton had given Hearts a two-goal lead inside the first 10 minutes, but goals from Andy Walker and Pat McGinlay ensured Hibs a share of the points they richly deserved from their second-half display.

His share of goals:
Hibernian's Pat McGinlay

A day later Celtic made a huge leap forward with their first league win against Rangers in eleven attempts. Goals from Craig Burley and Paul Lambert gaining the valuable points. The win kept Celtic in third place, but moved them to within just one point of their Glasgow rivals and the surprise of the season, Hearts. The Rangers goalkeeper, Andy Goram, kept the scores respectable on a night when Celtic looked invincible. To make things worse for Rangers, Paul Gascoigne was caught by the Sky TV camera pretending to play the flute in front of the Celtic supporters. The police were informed, but no action was to be taken if Rangers punished Gazza.

Big day for Celtic: Enrico Annoni crowds Rangers' Brian Laudrup as 'the Bhoys' go on to win 2–0

Monday March 8 1999

Tuesday March 9 1999

Wednesday March 10 1999

Thursday March 11 1999

Friday March 12 1999

Saturday March 13 1999
Dundee at Dunfermline Athletic

Sunday March 14 1999

Monday March 15 1999

Tuesday March 16 1999

Wednesday March 17 1999

Thursday March 18 1999

Friday March 19 1999

Saturday March 20 1999
St Johnstone at Dunfermline Athletic

Sunday March 21 1999

For the first time in 10 years Celtic overcame the steamroller that is Rangers. The win took Celtic to within a point of the league leaders with two well-taken goals. The only surprise was that it took Celtic so long to score their goals. The first was a great strike from Craig Burley after a great diagonal through ball by Jackie McNamara. Burley hit it first time and the ball was in the back of the net. The second goal was worthy of winning any Derby Game. Rangers had half-cleared a Celtic attack only for Lambert to hit a volley first time from 20 yards which flew past the despairing Andy Goram in the Rangers goal. The best chance of a result for Rangers came three minutes from the end when one of the floodlights above the North stand went out, but luckily for Celtic the rest of the lights did not go out.

Parkhead tussle: Celtic's Craig Burley and Rangers' Jonas Thern

The honours were shared in the Edinburgh derby after a revitalised Hibs asked serious questions about the sustainability of their closest rivals' championship quest. Kevin Harper's second-half display turned the game around for Hibs. Hearts had taken what looked like an unassailable lead after Steve Fulton had scored twice in the first 12 minutes. Whatever Hibs manager Jim Duffy said at half-time, it worked. Harper moved onto the right wing in the second half, and from here the face of the match changed. Hibs' first goal in the 51st minute came through an Andy Walker header after a cross from Fulton, and the second in the 62nd from Pat McGinlay. This was the first time that Hibs had gained a point from the Edinburgh derby in the last five games, but continued Hibs' terrible run of 16 games without a win.

Where are the wins? Hibee Andy Dow in action

Monday March 22 1999

Tuesday March 23 1999

Wednesday March 24 1999

Thursday March 25 1999

Friday March 26 1999

Saturday March 27 1999

Sunday March 28 1999

Monday March 29 1999

Tuesday March 30 1999

Wednesday March 31 1999

Thursday April 1 1999

Friday April 2 1999

Saturday April 3 1999
Dunfermline Athletic at Aberdeen

Sunday April 4 1999

The second week of January was tough for Paul Gascoigne, the Rangers midfielder, with the controversy over his flute-playing mime continuing to drag on. Rangers took the decision to fine Gazza £20,000 over the incident, for which he had to make a public apology. 'I would like to unreservedly apologise for my actions,' he said. He accepted that Rangers had made inroads into ending the old firm rivalry and his actions had done nothing to help this. In a further development Strathclyde police announced that Gascoigne had received a death threat which was described as 'the work of a crank'.

Level-headed:
The Jambos' Stephane Adam

Hearts moved back into second place in the Premier Division on 12 January after a superb performance by Jim Hamilton which kept their Championship hopes alive. Hamilton scored his first on 29 minutes and it looked to be easy for Hearts after Naysmith had made it 2–0 before half-time. After the break St Johnstone began to make a game of it and in the 63rd minute gained an equaliser from the penalty spot, but Hearts battled on. With three first team regulars missing, Hamilton scored the winner. The only downside to the game was that just 5,404 people turned up. Most stayed at home and watched the game live on Sky TV.

Flute playing does not pay: Rangers' Paul Gascoigne was fined £20,000 for a silly prank

Kilmarnock gained a point, but it should have been all three with great play in the second half against Hearts on 17 January. This was the third game between the two clubs this season and Hearts had won the previous two, but would have been pleased with the point to keep their title hopes alive... even if only just. They twice took the lead through Neil McCann on six minutes and later by an own goal from the Kilmarnock captain, Gus MacPherson, but Kilmarnock pegged Hearts back. After the shock of the midweek transfer of Dragoje Lekovic, the Kilmarnock goalkeeper, it looked as though it would be a bad end to a bad week, but goals from Paul Wright and Mark Reilly kept the Killie's unbeaten run alive.

New man in charge: Dick Advocaat, Rangers manager since 1 July this year

In the strongest indicator yet it appeared that Dick Advocaat would be appointed the manager of Rangers at the end of the season. Former manager, Graham Souness, said that he had been in contact with the Rangers hierarchy and it seemed that Dick Advocaat had the credentials that Rangers Chairman David Murray wanted. He had been successful with PSV and was in charge of the Dutch national side for a time. This rumour was later confirmed and Advocaat took over from Walter Smith on July 1st, 1998.

PHOTO NEWS SCOTLAND

Kilmarnock's Paul Wright: highest scoring native player in the Scottish PL

QUIZ 5 REFEREE QUIZ

1 According to FIFA, what is the minimum length of a pitch used in an international game?
- a) 90 metres
- b) 95 metres
- c) 100 metres

2 What is the acceptable pressure of a football?
- a) 0.6 to 1.1 atmospheres
- b) 0.5 to 1.25 atmospheres
- c) 0.75 to 2 atmospheres

3 Is the red attacking number 10 offside in this Diagram?

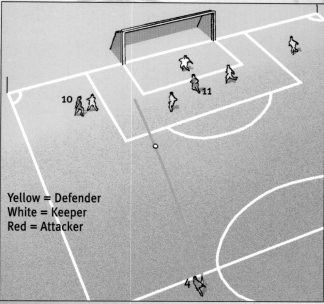

10

11

4

Yellow = Defender
White = Keeper
Red = Attacker

- a) No
- b) Yes
- c) Yes, but he's not interfering with play

4 When needs to go to penalties, who decides which end they are to be taken from?
- a) A toss of a coin before the game begins
- b) The referee decides
- c) A toss of a coin before the penalties are taken

5 If, during a penalty shoot-out, the keeper is injured and all substitutes have been used already, who replaces the keeper?
- a) A substitute keeper
- b) No one
- c) One of the outfield players

6 Your free-kick specialist takes a corner by flicking the ball in the air and curling it into the goal. What does the referee do?
- a) Awards the goal as fair
- b) Awards an indirect free-kick to the opposition (the corner taker is only allowed to touch the ball once until another player touches it).
- c) Awards a direct free-kick to the opposition (the corner taker is only allowed to touch the ball once until another player touches it).

7 Your keeper takes a free-kick but trips and the ball doesn't make it out of the area. What should the ref do?
- a) Has it taken again
- b) Allows play to continue
- c) Awards an indirect free-kick to the opposition

8 An opposition player persistently stands nose-to-nose with one of your team who is trying to take a throw-in, what should the referee do?
- a) Get the opposition player to stand 10-yards back
- b) Award an indirect free-kick to your team
- c) Caution the opposition player and give him a yellow card

9 What is the referee awarding in this Diagram?
- a) An indirect free-kick
- b) A corner
- c) A direct free-kick

10 If an indirect free-kick goes straight into the goal, what should the referee do?
- a) Have the kick re-taken
- b) Award an indirect free-kick to the opposition
- c) Award a goal kick

Monday April 5 1999

Tuesday April 6 1999

Wednesday April 7 1999

Thursday April 8 1999

Friday April 9 1999

Saturday April 10 1999
Dunfermline Athletic at Rangers

Sunday April 11 1999

Monday April 12 1999

Tuesday April 13 1999

Wednesday April 14 1999

Thursday April 15 1999

Friday April 16 1999

Saturday April 17 1999
Kilmarnock at Dunfermline Athletic   Scottish Cup semi-finals

Sunday April 18 1999

At the end of January Fergus McCann, Celtic managing director, and general manager Jock Brown launched a bid to remove some of the bigotry and intolerance in Scottish Football. Working with church, educational and media representatives, the aim of the campaign was to teach 'respect, tolerance and understanding'. Celtic had already moved against sectarianism by banning people from their ground if found guilty of involvement. The move backfired later in the week when Celtic 'old bhoys' Tommy Burns and David Hay were branded as bigots by McCann after they said the club was moving away from its traditional roots.

Celtic player Simon Donelly in action

In the Third Round of the Scottish Cup there was only one shock result, but a number of lower division clubs gave a good account of themselves. The surprise came at Fir Park where Hibernian were comfortably beaten 2–1 by an impressive Raith Rovers. Nearly the biggest surprise of the day was at Hamilton where it took a 90th-minute Richard Gough goal to give Rangers a lucky 2–1 victory, but both Hearts and Celtic won 2–0 to go into the draw for the fourth round. In the only all-Premier Division tie between Dundee United and Aberdeen a Robbie Winters goal meant that Aberdeen were knocked out of the competition. The cup holders Kilmarnock also came through 2–0 against Stranraer.

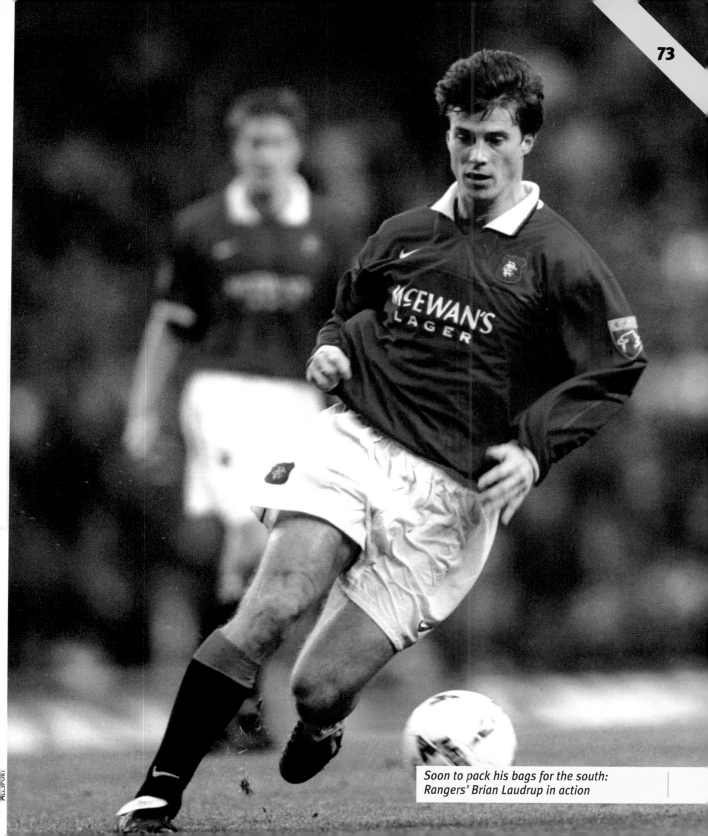

Soon to pack his bags for the south: Rangers' Brian Laudrup in action

Monday April 19 1999

Tuesday April 20 1999

Wednesday April 21 1999

Thursday April 22 1999

Friday April 23 1999

Saturday April 24 1999
Dundee United at Dunfermline Athletic

Sunday April 25 1999

Monday April 26 1999

Tuesday April 27 1999

Wednesday April 28 1999

Thursday April 29 1999

Friday April 30 1999

Saturday May 1 1999
Dunfermline Athletic at Heart of Midlothian

Sunday May 2 1999

On 2 February, bottom-of-the-table club Hibernian sacked Jim Duffy after 13 months as their manager. Over the last few weeks their results had steadily got worse; they had only one win in their last 19 games. Hibs lost their last game with Duffy in charge 6–2 to Motherwell after taking a one-goal lead inside eight minutes. The week before they had been unceremoniously dumped out of the cup by First Division Raith Rovers. Duffy left the Easter Road side four points adrift at the bottom of the Premier League. The assistant manager Jackie McNamara was also fired. It was announced that Billy McNeill would move from his job as director of development to become the caretaker manager.

Black February:
Jim Duffy, sacked manager of Hibs

St Johnstone did it again. After beating Celtic earlier in the season they did it to the other Auld Firm team, beating Rangers 2–0 at McDiarmid Park. Goals from John O'Neil and George O'Boyle in the 36th and 69th minute respectively gave the Perth side the points. It was the first time in 50 games and 27 years that St Johnstone had beaten the Glasgow side. Walter Smith, the Rangers manager, said it was a lacklustre performance, and could not understand why his team didn't seem to settle into the game until the opposition had got into their stride. The result left the championship race wide open, with Rangers, Celtic and Hearts all in with a shout of being crowned champions in May.

St Johnstone v Rangers 31/1/98:
Rangers' Joachim Bjorkland and Gordan Petric

Monday May 3 1999

Tuesday May 4 1999

Wednesday May 5 1999

Thursday May 6 1999

Friday May 7 1999

Saturday May 8 1999
Celtic at Dunfermline Athletic

Sunday May 9 1999

Monday May 10 1999

Tuesday May 11 1999

Wednesday May 12 1999

Thursday May 13 1999

Friday May 14 1999

Saturday May 15 1999
Dunfermline Athletic at Dundee

Sunday May 16 1999

Alex McLeish was named the new manager of Hibernian on 12 February. The former Scottish international defender moved to Hibs from Motherwell, themselves at the wrong end of the table. Strangely it was Hibs' 6–2 defeat by Motherwell under the charge of McLeish that led to the sacking of Duffy. There was a lot of behind-the-scenes discussion between Hibernian and Motherwell over the issue of compensation, but that was ironed out and McLeish took over for his first game in charge against Rangers in the Scottish Cup. McLeish also took assistant manager Andy Watson and coach Jim Griffin with him to Easter Road.

John Robertson of Hearts in action

After five months of legal battles, the ten breakaway clubs finally got what they wanted, a new Scottish Premier division. It took less than one hour for the 30 lower division clubs to agree to let the big ten split. The main result was that the top clubs would now be free to negotiate their own TV rights deals which many believed would mean 'pay-to-view' schemes would become the norm. There was no doubt about the result of the vote. The months of discussion and the £1.7 million per year that the lower divisions had been promised swung it, and the resolution was passed with 58 votes for and 20 against.

Wayward, but inspirational: Hibernian's midfielder, Chic Charnley

Monday May 17 1999

Tuesday May 18 1999

Wednesday May 19 1999

Thursday May 20 1999

Friday May 21 1999

Saturday May 22 1999
Motherwell at Dunfermline Athletic

Sunday May 23 1999

Monday May 24 1999

Tuesday May 25 1999

Wednesday May 26 1999

Thursday May 27 1999

Friday May 28 1999

Saturday May 29 1999
Scottish Cup Final

Sunday May 30 1999

Kjell Olofsson spared Dundee United blushes as he scored an 81st minute equaliser against Second Division Caledonian Thistle on Valentine's day. Thistle had taken a shock lead in the 26th minute through Paul Sheerin, but from there on in it was all Dundee United. Jim Calder, the Thistle goalkeeper, was deservedly voted Man of the Match with a string of wonderful saves. United also made life hard for themselves with Gary McSwegan, playing in place of Robbie Winters, missing a whole host of easy chances. Thistle then went on to prove that the result was no fluke in the replay. A breathless game finished 3–2 to United after extra time with a Zutterland goal in the 108th minute of the game. Thistle finished the game with a great deal of pride and did their division proud.

Club captain David Bowman watches as Lars Zetterlund makes his play

It was the start of a good week for Celtic. They moved to the top of the league and their newest import, Harald Brattbakk, a £2.5 million signing from Rosenburg earlier in the season, started to hit the back of the net. He had not scored in his first six games for the club, but then showed the Celtic fans what he could do with a devastating display of finishing against Kilmarnock. In the end he could have had seven or eight after hitting the post twice and being unlucky to miss on three other occasions. Brattbakk followed this later in the week with two goals against Dunfermline Athletic in Celtic's 5–1 win.

Celtic's Harald Brattbakk: not as successful at scoring as had been hoped...

PHOTO NEWS SCOTLAND

Celebration time for victorious Falkirk

The shock of the quarter-finals of the Scottish Cup came when First Division promotion hopefuls Falkirk destroyed St Johnstone 3–0 on 7 March. This was a game that the men of St Johnstone would have expected to win, but they were well-beaten. Falkirk took the lead through a Seaton goal in the first half and two goals either side of half-time from Moss. Falkirk were rarely in trouble, especially after they went 3–0 up, and their reward for their brilliant performance was a semi-final appearance against the team second in the League table, Heart of Midlothian.

Wim Jansen, the Celtic head coach, made a shock announcement that he might leave the club at the end of the season. In a message on Celtic's official supporters' hotline he announced that he had a clause in his three-year contract that would allow him to leave in July if he wanted to. Jansen had been a revelation this past year for Celtic, giving them a real chance of doing the Triple. He was reported as saying he wanted to see out his contract, but at this stage had not made up his mind yet.

QUIZ 6 ABOUT SCOTTISH PREMIER LEAGUE

1 Against which club did the Hibernian keeper score a goal in a Premier Division match in 1988?
a) Hearts
b) Aberdeen
c) Morton

2 The biggest Premier Division win occurred in March 1979 when Aberdeen beat Motherwell. What was the score?
a) 8–0
b) 10–0
c) 12–0

3 Which is the only club to have scored 100 goals in a Premier Division season?
a) Celtic
b) Aberdeen
c) Rangers

4 Which is the only club to have conceded 100 goals in a Premier Division season?
a) Hamilton Academicals
b) Dunfermline Athletic
c) Morton

5 For how many games was Duncan Ferguson banned for violent conduct in 1994?
a) Five
b) Nine
c) Twelve

6 Who was Scottish Manager of the Year in 1990?
a) Andy Roxbrugh
b) Graeme Souness
c) Walter Smith

7 Celtic beat Hamilton in the Premier Division in January 1987 by what score?
a) 7–4
b) 8–3
c) 9–2

8 How many times did Celtic score when the two teams met again the following year?
a) Six
b) Seven
c) Eight

9 When was the first Premier Division season?
a) 1973-74
b) 1975-76
c) 1977-78

10 Who was the first player to score 200 goals in the Premier Division?
a) Ally McCoist
b) Mo Johnston
c) Gordon Durie

From derision to hero worship: the changing attitudes to Celtic head coach Wim Jansen

Answers: 1.c 2.a 3.c 4.c 5.c 6.a 7.b 8.b 9.b 10.a

Monday May 31 1999

Tuesday June 1 1999

Wednesday June 2 1999

Thursday June 3 1999

Friday June 4 1999

Saturday June 5 1999

Sunday June 6 1999

Monday June 7 1999

Tuesday June 8 1999

Wednesday June 9 1999

Thursday June 10 1999

Friday June 11 1999

Saturday June 12 1999

Sunday June 13 1999

After weeks of speculation, offers and counter-offers, the rumours of Paul Gascoigne's move from Rangers were ended at the end of March. It was first believed that Gazza would go to English relegation strugglers Crystal Palace, but in the end he went to Middlesbrough for £3.45 million. He decided that he was no longer needed in Glasgow and that the time to move on had come. He would go straight into the Middlesbrough team for the Coca-Cola Cup Final even though he had not played a great deal of first team football at Rangers since Christmas.

End of the road: Gazza's last appearance for Rangers

Falkirk put up a brilliant display in their semi-final against Hearts. They could consider themselves very unfortunate to have been knocked out after playing the better football. It was supposed to be a one-sided semi-final, but not with Falkirk having the upper hand! Hearts scored with their first real opportunity, but from then on it was all Falkirk, and they equalised on 85 minutes through Kevin McAllister. It seemed that the reply was on, a well-needed money earner for Falkirk who went into voluntary receivership only a few weeks before, but it was not to be. Hearts scored two goals in the last minute to gain an undeserved victory. In the other semi-final Rangers beat Celtic 2–1.

Part of the east coast challenge to the Auld Firm: Stephane Adam of Hearts of Midlothian

Monday June 14 1999

Tuesday June 15 1999

Wednesday June 16 1999

Thursday June 17 1999

Friday June 18 1999

Saturday June 19 1999   Sunday June 20 1999

Monday June 21 1999

Tuesday June 22 1999

Wednesday June 23 1999

Thursday June 24 1999

Friday June 25 1999

Saturday June 26 1999   Sunday June 27 1999

On 11 April, Jim Hamilton, the Heart of Midlothian striker, was given a three-match ban after his yellow card at Easter Road in the Edinburgh derby against Hibernian. He was given the card by referee Willie Young for feigning injury after a touchline incident involving Pat McGinlay where Hamilton pretended to be elbowed in the face. The ban meant he would miss games against Rangers, Aberdeen and Dunfermline although he would play against St Johnstone and in the Scottish Cup Final on May 16.

Gilles Rousset, from Olympique Marseille to Hearts – a good move

Hearts' league championship challenge may have faded over the last month of the season, but their only chance of silverware this season, the Scottish Cup, also looked out of their reach in the dress rehearsal of that final on 25 April. Rangers dominated from the kick-off and never looked like losing. The only surprise of the game was that it took 48 minutes for Rangers to score their opening goal. The first came from Rino Gattuso, who went on to score a second, and finally a third for Rangers on 78 minutes. The other came from Jorg Albertz. Rangers did not field their strongest side and won the game with room to spare. The Cup did not look like it was going to Tynecastle.

*Still on top: Celtic's Lambert and the Gers'
Drurie in the 2–0 win for Rangers on 12/4/98*

Monday June 28 1999

Tuesday June 29 1999

Wednesday June 30 1999

Thursday July 1 1999

Friday July 2 1999

Saturday July 3 1999

Sunday July 4 1999

ACTION IMAGES

Two scorers and the Scottish FA Cup: Colin Cameron and Stephane Adam

If Celtic had won at Dunfermline on 3 May, the championship would have been theirs. Instead the title race tensely moved into another week. After a great first half, in which Celtic had a hatful of chances, they could only manage one well-taken goal from Simon Donnelly. As the game moved into the later stages of the second half Celtic began to get more and more nervous. Then on 82 minutes the inevitable happened. Craig Faulconbridge, a second-half substitute, came on and put a looping header past Jonathon Gould in the Celtic goal to equalise. The championship race was still on with Rangers not out of it yet.

On 9 May, in scenes of great celebration, Tommy Boyd lifted the Championship trophy for Celtic for the first time in 10 years. It was secured after a nervous 2–0 win over St Johnstone, with goals from Henrik Larsson and Harald Brattbakk. The score flattered to deceive, but the fans and the players didn't care once the final whistle came. The celebrations were short lived – only two days later Wim Jansen told the Celtic board that he would not take the second year extension on his contract and would leave Celtic with immediate effect. It had been a very strange and exciting season for them.

Rangers finished the season without a trophy and Hearts finished with one for the first time in 36 years. Hearts took the lead on 16 May within one minute when Ian Ferguson brought down Hearts captain Steve Fulton in the box for a penalty. Colin Cameron stepped up to beat Andy Goram from the spot. Rangers were always in the match – Brian Laudrup hit the post and Lorenzo Amoruso came close with a free kick from 40 yards out. But it was Hearts' turn next when Frenchman Stephane Adam scored in the 58th minute. Rangers again rallied and Ally McCoist, in maybe his last game, scored with nine minutes left. Rangers pressed but could not score the vital equaliser and Hearts got the Scottish Cup. It was a disappointing season for Walter Smith, but even he could not deny Hearts some silverware for their brilliant season.

At last: Celtic's Tom Boyd and Harald Brattbakk
dress up and cheer with the Premiership trophy

		DATE	SCORE	POINTS	PLACE	SCORERS
Dunfermline Athletic .v . . . . Aberdeen	HOME	/ /	–			
	AWAY	/ /	–			
Dunfermline Athletic .v . . . . Celtic	HOME	/ /	–			
	AWAY	/ /	–			
Dunfermline Athletic .v . . . . Dundee	HOME	/ /	–			
	AWAY	/ /	–			
Dunfermline Athletic .v . . . . . Dundee United	HOME	/ /	–			
	AWAY	/ /	–			
Dunfermline Athletic .v . Heart of Midlothian	HOME	/ /	–			
	AWAY	/ /	–			
Dunfermline Athletic .v . . . . Kilmarnock	HOME	/ /	–			
	AWAY	/ /	–			
Dunfermline Athletic .v . . . . Motherwell	HOME	/ /	–			
	AWAY	/ /	–			
Dunfermline Athletic .v . . . . Rangers	HOME	/ /	–			
	AWAY	/ /	–			
Dunfermline Athletic .v . . . . St Johnstone	HOME	/ /	–			
	AWAY	/ /	–			

NOTES

		DATE	SCORE	POINTS	PLACE	SCORERS
Dunfermline Athletic .v . . . . Aberdeen	HOME	/ /	–			
	AWAY	/ /	–			
Dunfermline Athletic .v . . . . Celtic	HOME	/ /	–			
	AWAY	/ /	–			
Dunfermline Athletic .v . . . . Dundee	HOME	/ /	–			
	AWAY	/ /	–			
Dunfermline Athletic .v . . . . . Dundee United	HOME	/ /	–			
	AWAY	/ /	–			
Dunfermline Athletic .v . Heart of Midlothian	HOME	/ /	–			
	AWAY	/ /	–			
Dunfermline Athletic .v . . . . Kilmarnock	HOME	/ /	–			
	AWAY	/ /	–			
Dunfermline Athletic .v . . . . Motherwell	HOME	/ /	–			
	AWAY	/ /	–			
Dunfermline Athletic .v . . . . Rangers	HOME	/ /	–			
	AWAY	/ /	–			
Dunfermline Athletic .v . . . . St Johnstone	HOME	/ /	–			
	AWAY	/ /	–			

NOTES

SUPPORTERS' AWAY INFORMATION

UNITED KINGDOM AIRPORTS

Aberdeen (Dyce)	01224 722331
Belfast (Aldegrove)	01849 422888
Birmingham International	0121 767-5511
Blackpool	01253 343434
Bournemouth (Hurn)	01202 593939
Bristol (Luisgate)	01275 474444
Cambridge	01223 61133
Cardiff	01446 711211
East Midlands	01332 852852
Edinburgh	0131333-1000
Glasgow	0141 887 1111
Humberside	01652 688491
Inverness (Dalcross)	01463 232471
Leeds & Bradford (Yeadon)	01132 509696
Liverpool (Speke)	0151 486-8877
London (Gatwick)	01293 535353
London (Heathrow)	0181 759-4321
London (London City)	0171 474-5555
London (Stanstead)	01279 680500
Luton	01582 405100
Lydd	01797 320401
Manchester (Ringway)	0161 489-3000
Newcastle (Woolsington)	0191 286-0966
Newquay (St. Mawgan)	01637 860551
Norwich	01603 411923
Plymouth	01752 772752
Prestwick	01292 479822
Southampton	01703 629600
Southend	01702 340201
Stornoway	01851 702256
Teesside (Darlington)	01325 332811
Westland Heliport	0171 228-0181

TOURIST & TRAVEL INFORMATION CENTRES

ENGLAND

Birmingham (NEC)	0121 780-4321
Blackpool	01253 21623
Bournemouth	01202 789789
Brighton	01273 323755
Cambridge	01223 322640
Chester	01244 351609
Colchester	01206 282920
Dover	01304 205108
Durham	0191 384-3720
Hull	01482 223559
Lancaster	01524 32878
Leicester	01162 650555
Lincoln	01522 529828
Liverpool	0151 708-8838
Manchester	0161 234-3157
Newcastle-upon-Tyne	0191 261-0691
Newquay	01603 871345
Norwich	01603 666071
Oxford	01865 726871
Portsmouth	01705 826722
Southampton	01703 221106
Torquay	01803 297428
York	01904 620557

SCOTLAND

Aberdeen	01224 632727
Edinburgh	0131 557-1700
Glasgow	0141 848-4440
Stirling	01786 475019

WALES

Cardiff	01222 227281
Wrexham	01978 292015

PASSPORT OFFICES

London	0171 799-2728

Clive House, 70–78 Petty France, SW1H 9HD

Liverpool	0151 237-3010

5th Floor, India Buildings, Water Street, L2 0QZ

Peterborough	01733 555688

UK Passport Agency, Aragon Court,
Northminster Road, Peterborough PE1 1QG

Glasgow	0141 332-4441

3 Northgate, 96 Milton Street, Cowcadens,
Glasgow G4 0BT

Newport	01633 473700

Olympia House, Upper Dock Street, Newport,
Gwent NP9 1XQ

Belfast	01232 330214

Hampton House, 47–53 High Street,
Belfast BT1 2QS

MAIN INTER-CITY RAIL CONNECTIONS FOR
SCOTLAND

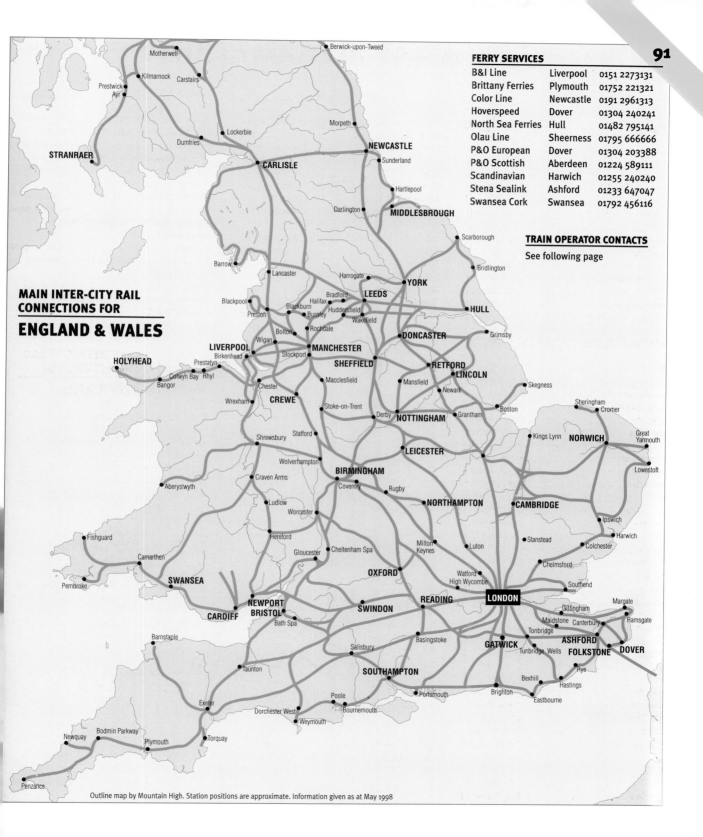

MAIN INTER-CITY RAIL CONNECTIONS FOR

ENGLAND & WALES

FERRY SERVICES

B&I Line	Liverpool	0151 2273131
Brittany Ferries	Plymouth	01752 221321
Color Line	Newcastle	0191 2961313
Hoverspeed	Dover	01304 240241
North Sea Ferries	Hull	01482 795141
Olau Line	Sheerness	01795 666666
P&O European	Dover	01304 203388
P&O Scottish	Aberdeen	01224 589111
Scandinavian	Harwich	01255 240240
Stena Sealink	Ashford	01233 647047
Swansea Cork	Swansea	01792 456116

TRAIN OPERATOR CONTACTS

See following page

STRANRAER

Motherwell
Kilmarnock   Carstairs
Prestwick
Ayr
Dumfries   Lockerbie

Berwick-upon-Tweed

Morpeth

CARLISLE   NEWCASTLE
Sunderland

Hartlepool

Darlington   MIDDLESBROUGH

Scarborough

Barrow

Bridlington

Lancaster   Harrogate   YORK

Blackpool   Bradford   LEEDS
Preston   Blackburn   Halifax   Huddersfield   HULL
Burnley   Wakefield

Bolton   Rochdale   Grimsby
Wigan   DONCASTER

HOLYHEAD   LIVERPOOL   Birkenhead   MANCHESTER
Prestatyn   Stockport   SHEFFIELD   RETFORD
Colwyn Bay   Rhyl   Macclesfield   Mansfield   LINCOLN
Bangor   Chester   Newark
Skegness

Wrexham   CREWE   Stoke-on-Trent   Sheringham
Derby   NOTTINGHAM   Boston   Cromer

Shrewsbury   Stafford   Grantham

Aberystwyth   Wolverhampton   LEICESTER   Kings Lynn   NORWICH
Great Yarmouth

Craven Arms   BIRMINGHAM   Lowestoft
Coventry   Rugby

Ludlow   NORTHAMPTON   CAMBRIDGE
Worcester   Ipswich
Hereford   Harwich
Milton   Luton   Stansted   Colchester
Fishguard   Keynes

Camarthen   Gloucester   Cheltenham Spa   Chelmsford

SWANSEA   OXFORD   Watford   Southend
Pembroke   High Wycombe

NEWPORT   READING   LONDON   Margate
CARDIFF   BRISTOL   SWINDON   Gillingham   Ramsgate
Bath Spa   Maidstone   Canterbury
Tonbridge

Barnstaple   Basingstoke   GATWICK   ASHFORD
Salisbury   Tunbridge Wells   FOLKSTONE   DOVER
Taunton   Rye
Bexhill   Hastings
SOUTHAMPTON   Brighton   Eastbourne
Poole   Portsmouth
Exeter   Bournemouth
Dorchester West   Weymouth

Newquay   Bodmin Parkway
Plymouth   Torquay

Penzance

SUPPORTERS' AWAY INFORMATION

TRAIN OPERATORS

ANGLIA RAILWAYS
15-25 Artillery Lane, London, E1 7HA
Tel 01473 693333
Fax 01473 693497

CARDIFF RAILWAY CO
10th Floor, Brunel House, 2 Fitzalan Rd,
Cardiff CF2 1SA
Tel 01222 430000
Fax 01222 480463

CENTRAL TRAINS
PO Box 4323, Stanier House, 10 Holliday Street
Birmingham B1 1TH
Tel 0121 654 4444
Fax 0121 654 4461

CHILTERN RAILWAY CO
Western House, 14 Rickfords Hill, Aylesbury
HP20 2RX
Tel 01296 332100
Fax 01296 332126

CONNEX SOUTH CENTRAL
Stephenson House, 2 Cherry Orchard Road,
Croydon CR9 6JB
Tel 0181 667 2780
Fax 0181 667 2906

EUROSTAR (UK)
Eurostar House, Waterloo Station, London
SE1 8SE
Tel 0171 928 5151

GATWICK EXPRESS
52 Grosvenor Gardens, London SW1W 0AU
Tel 0171 973 5005
Fax 0171 973 5038

GREAT EASTERN RAILWAY
Hamilton House, 3 Appold Street, London
EC2A 2AA
Tel 0645 50 50 00
Fax 01473 693745

GREAT NORTH EATERN RAILWAY
Main Headquarters Building, York YO1 1HT
Tel 01904 653022
Fax 01904 523392

GREAT WESTERN TRAINS CO
Milford House, 1 Milton Street, Swindon SN1 1HL
Tel 01793 499400
Fax 01793 499460

HEATHROW EXPRESS
4th Floor, Cardinal Point, Newall Rd, Hounslow
Middlesex TW6 2QS
Tel 0181 745 0578
Fax 0181 745 1627

ISLAND LINE
Ryde St Johns Road Station, Ryde, Isle Of Wight
PO33 2BA
Tel 01983 812591
Fax 01983 817879

LTS RAIL
Central House, Clifftown Road, Southend-on-Sea
SS1 1AB
Tel 01702 357889

MERSEYRAIL ELECTRICS
Rail House, Lord Nelson Street, Liverpool L1 1JF
Tel 0151 709 8292
Fax 0151 702 2413

MIDLAND MAINLINE
Midland House, Nelson Street, Derby,
East Midlands DE1 2SA
Tel 0345 221125
Fax 01332 262011

NORTH WESTERN TRAINS
PO Box 44, Rail House, Store Street
Manchester M60 1DQ
Tel 0161 228 2141
Fax 0161 228 5003

REGIONAL RAILWAYS NORTH EAST
Main Headquarters Building, York YO1 1HT
Tel 01904 653022

SCOTRAIL RAILWAYS
Caledonian Chambers, 87 Union Street
Glasgow G1 3TA
Tel 0141 332 9811

SILVERLINK TRAIN SERVICES
65-67 Clarendon Raod, Watford WD1 1DP
Tel 01923 207258
Fax 01923 207023

SOUTH WEST TRAINS
Friars Bridge Court, 41-45 Blackfrairs Road
London SE1 8NZ
Tel 0171 928 5151
Fax 0171 902 3208

THAMESLINK RAIL
Friars Bridge, 41-45 Blackfriars Road,
London SE1 8NZ
Tel 0171 620 5760
Fax 0171 620 5099

THAMES TRAINS
Venture House, 37 Blagrave Street, Reading
RG1 1PZ
Tel 0118 908 3678
Fax 0118 957 9006

VIRGIN TRAINS
85 Smallbrook Queensway, Birmingham B5 4HA
Tel 0121 654 7400
Fax 0121 654 7487

WALES & WEST
Brunel House, 2 Fitzalan Rd, Cardiff CF2 1SU
Tel 01222 430400
Fax 01222 430214

WEST ANGLIA GREAT NORTHERN RAILWAY
Hertford House, 1 Cranwood Street, London
EC1V 9GT
Tel 0345 818919
Fax 01223 453606

WEST COAST RAILWAY COMPANY
Warton Road, Carnforth, Lancashire LA5 9HX
Tel 01524 732100
Fax 01524 735518

SOCCER RELATED INTERNET BOOKMARKS

The following three pages are a listing of soccer websites, some of which you may find useful to bookmark. As any internet browser will know all too well, URLs change, move or become obsolete at the drop of a hat. At the time of going to press all the ones listed were active.

If you are new to internet browsing, the following information on entering the URL addresses should be observed. Because of the way the address lines are printed, those longer than the width of the column are broken into two lines, second slightly indented. Nevertheless, all the characters of the address should be typed in as one line, with no spaces between characters. If your edition or version of browser already enters the 'http://' characters, or does not require them, omit these from the URL address.

Where sites are official, it states so in brackets after the site name. Any useful notes about the site are given after the name in square brackets.

WORLD CUP RELATED PAGES

Football Web in Japan
http://www.nidnet.com/link/socweb.html
CBS SportsLine - Soccer
http://www.sportsline.com/u/soccer/index.
html
Teams of the World
http://www.islandia.is/totw/
World Cup - Soccernet
http://www.soccernet.com/u/soccer/world
cup98/index.html
World Cup 1998 - CBS SportsLine
http://www.sportsline.com/u/soccer/world
cup98/qualifying/index.html
**World Cup Soccer - France 98 - Coupe du
Monde**
http://www.worldcup.com/english/index.
html

FOOTBALL RELATED

1997 edition of the Laws of the Game
http://www.fifa.com/fifa/handbook/laws/
index.laws.html
Soccer Books [good reference]
http://www.soccer-books.co.uk
British Society of Sports History [reference
material]
http://www.umist.ac.uk/UMIST_Sport/bssh.
html
Buchanan Brigade Messge Bd Thirty-Three
http://www.buchanan.org/mb33.html
Communicata Football
http://www.communicata.co.uk/lookover/
football/
Division 1 Web Pages [relates to the
Nationwide leagues]
http://www.users.globalnet.co.uk/~emmas/
ndiv1.htm
Division 2 Web Pages [old Endsleigh rather
than the Nationwide]
http://www.uwm.edu/People/dyce/htfc/
clubs/div2-www.html
England [Engerland]
http://www.users.dircon.co.uk/~england/
england/
England [Green Flags England team pages]
http://www.greenflag.co.uk/te/fslist.html
England [English Soccernet - National Team
- News]
http://www.soccernet.com/english/national/
news/index.html
England
http://www.englandfc.com/
English Club Homepages
http://pluto.webbernet.net/~bob/engclub.
html
FAI - Irish International
http://www.fai.ie/
GeordieSport!
http://www.geordiepride.demon.co.uk/
geordiesport.htm
L & M Referees' Society - Soccer Pages
http://www.lancs.ac.uk/ug/williams/soccer.
htm
Northern Ireland [Norn Iron!: The NI
International Football 'zine]
http://students.un.umist.ac.uk/gbh/index.
html
Notts Association
http://www.innotts.co.uk/~soccerstats/

gallery/nmf8.htm
Scotland [Rampant Scotland - Sport]
http://scotland.rampant.com/sport.htm
Scotland
http://web.city.ac.uk/~sh393/euro/scotland.
htm
Scottish Football Association (Official)
http://www.scottishfa.co.uk/
Scottish Mailing Lists
http://www.isfa.com/isfa/lists/scotland.htm
Simply the Best
http://www.int-foot-fame.com/famers1.htm
Soccer ScoreSheet History List
http://www.kazmax.demon.co.uk/websheet/
tm000309.htm
Soccer-Tables
http://www.marwin.ch/sport/fb/index.e.
html
SoccerSearch: Players:G-P
http://www.soccersearch.com/Players/G-P/
SoccerSpace, Football & Soccer Links
http://www.winbet.sci.fi/soccerspace/links.
htm
Team England - Fixtures & Results
http://ourworld.compuserve.com/homepages
/nic_king/england/fixtures.htm
The Association of Football Statisticians
http://www.innotts.co.uk/~soccerstats/
**The Aylesbury Branch of the Referees'
Association**
http://homepages.bucks.net/~bigmick/
The Daily Soccer
http://www.dailysoccer.com/
The Football Supporters' Association (FSA)
http://www.fsa.org.uk
US Soccer History Archives
http://www.sover.net/~spectrum/index.html
**Welsh Football,Football wales,faw,welsh
fa,ryan giggs**
http://www.citypages.co.uk/faw/

ENGLISH PREMIERSHIP

Arsenal
http://www.arsenal.co.uk/
Aston Villa
http://www.geocities.com/Colosseum/Field/
6089/
Aston Villa
http://www.villan.demon.co.uk/
Aston Villa
http://www.gbar.dtu.dk/~c937079/AVFC/
index.html
Aston Villa (Official)
http://www.gbar.dtu.dk/~c937079/CB/
Barnsley
http://www.geocities.com/Colosseum/Field/
6059/bfc.html
Barnsley
http://www.u-net.com/westex/bfc.htm
Barnsley
http://www.radders.skynet.co.uk/
Barnsley
http://upload.virgin.net/d.penty/
Copacabarnsley/Copacabarnsley.htm
Barnsley
http://members.aol.com/JLister/bfc/bfc.htm
Blackburn Rovers
http://www.brfc-supporters.org.uk/
Blackburn Rovers (Official)
http://www.rovers.co.uk/
Bolton Wanderers
http://www.hankins.demon.co.uk/bwscl/
index.html

Bolton Wanderers
http://www.netcomuk.co.uk/~cjw/football.
html
Bolton Wanderers
http://www.geocities.com/Colosseum/4433/
Bolton Wanderers
http://mail.freeway.co.uk/druid/
Bolton Wanderers (Official)
http://www.boltonwfc.co.uk/
Charlton Athletic
http://www.demon.co.uk/casc/index.html
Chelsea
http://www.geocities.com/Colosseum/1457/
chelsea.html
Chelsea
http://web.ukonline.co.uk/Members/jf.
lettice/cfcmain.html
Chelsea
http://www.jack.dircon.net/chelsea/
Chelsea
http://fans-of.chelsea-fc.com/csr/
Chelsea FC (Official)
http://www.chelseafc.co.uk/chelsea/
frontpage.shtml
Coventry City [mpegs of goals... that's it]
http://karpaty.tor.soliton.com/ccfcgoals/
Coventry City [The Sky Blue Superplex]
http://www.geocities.com/TimesSquare/
Dungeon/1641/page4.html
Coventry City
http://www.warwick.ac.uk/~cudbu/SkyBlues.
html
Coventry City (Official)
http://www.ccfc.co.uk/
Derby County
http://lard.sel.cam.ac.uk/derby_county/
Derby County
http://www.cheme.cornell.edu/~jwillits/this.
html
Derby County
http://easyweb.easynet.co.uk/~nickwheat/
ramsnet.html
Derby County
http://home.sol.no/~einasand/derby.htm
Derby County
http://www.cheme.cornell.edu/~jwillits/
derby2.html#History
Derby County
http://www.derby-county.com/main.htm
Derby County (Official)
http://www.dcfc.co.uk/dcfc/index.html
Everton FC (Official)
http://www.connect.org.uk/everton/
Leeds United
http://www.lufc.co.uk/
Leeds United
http://spectrum.tcns.co.uk/cedar/leeds.htm
Leeds United
http://www.csc.liv.ac.uk/users/tim/Leeds/
Leeds United (Official - CarlingNet)
http://www.fa-premier.com/club/lufc/
Leicester City (Official)
http://www.lcfc.co.uk/141097b.htm
Liverpool
http://akureyri.ismennt.is/~jongeir/
Liverpool
http://www.soccernet.com/livrpool/
Liverpool
http://www.connect.org.uk/anfield/
Manchester United
http://www.cs.indiana.edu/hyplan/ccheah/
posts.html
Manchester United
http://www.geocities.com/SouthBeach/6367

/index.html
Manchester United
http://www.sky.co.uk/sports/manu/
Manchester United
http://www.cybernet.dk/users/barrystorv/
Manchester United
http://home.pacific.net.sg/~jerping/
Manchester United
http://sunhehi.phy.uic.edu/~clive/MUFC/
home.html
Manchester United
http://www.iol.ie/~mmurphy/red_devils/
mufc.htm
Manchester United
http://www.davewest.demon.co.uk/
Manchester United
http://www.webcom.com/~solution/mufc/
manu.html
Manchester United
http://ourworld.compuserve.com/homepages
/red_devil/
Manchester United
http://xanadu.centrum.is/~runarhi/
Manchester United
http://web.city.ac.uk/~sh393/mufc.htm
Manchester United
http://www.wsu.edu:8080/~mmarks/Giggs.
html
Manchester United
http://osiris.sunderland.ac.uk/online/access
/manutd/redshome.html
Manchester United
http://www.u-net.com/~pitman/
Manchester United
http://www.geocities.com/Colosseum/2483/
Manchester United
http://www.wsu.edu:8080/~mmarks/
mufclinks.html
Manchester United
http://gladstone.uoregon.edu:80/~jsetzen/
mufc.html
Manchester United
http://members.hknet.com/~siukin/
Newcastle United
http://www.swan.co.uk/TOTT
Newcastle United
http://www.nufc.com
Newcastle United
http://www.btinternet.com/~the.magpie/
history1.htm
Newcastle United
http://www.ccacyber.com/nufc/
Newcastle United
http://sunflower.singnet.com.sg/~resa21/
Nottingham Forest
http://users.homenet.ie/~aidanhut/
Nottingham Forest
http://www.thrustworld.co.uk/users/kryten/
forest/
Nottingham Forest
http://hem1.passagen.se/pearce/index.htm
Nottingham Forest
http://www.innotts.co.uk/~joe90/forest.htm
Nottingham Forest
http://ourworld.compuserve.com/homepages
/kencrossland/
Nottingham Forest (Official)
http://www.nottingham-
forest.co.uk/frames.html
Sheffield Wednesday
http://www.crg.cs.nott.ac.uk/Users/anb/
Football/stats/swfcarch.htm
Sheffield Wednesday
http://www.rhi.hi.is/~jbj/sheffwed/opnun.htm

BOOKMARKS

Sheffield Wednesday
http://www.geocities.com/Colosseum/2938/
Sheffield Wednesday
http://www.cs.nott.ac.uk/~anb/Football/
Southampton [Saintsweb]
http://www.soton.ac.uk/~saints/
Southampton [Marching In]
http://www.saintsfans.com/marchingin/
Tottenham Hotspur [White Hart Site]
http://www.xpress.se/~ssab0019/webring/
index.html
Tottenham Hotspur [Felix Gills' Page]
http://www.gilnet.demon.co.uk/spurs.htm
Tottenham Hotspur
http://www.personal.u-net.com/~spurs/
Tottenham Hotspur [check Spurs results
year-by-year - just stats]
http://www.bobexcell.demon.co.uk/
Tottenham Hotspur
http://www.btinternet.com/~matt.cook
Tottenham Hotspur (Official)
http://www.spurs.co.uk/welcome.html
West Ham United
http://www.ecs.soton.ac.uk/saints/premier/
westham.htm
West Ham United
http://www.westhamunited.co.uk/
Wimbledon
http://www.fa-premier.com/cgi-bin/
fetch/club/wfc/home.html?team='WIM'
Wimbledon [unofficial - WISA]
http://www.wisa.org.uk/
Wimbledon [Womble.Net - Independent
Wimbledon FC Internet 'zine]
http://www.geocities.com/SunsetStrip/
Studio/6112/womblnet.html
Wimbledon [very basic]
http://www.aracnet.com/~davej/football.
htm
Wimbledon [unofficial - USA]
http://soyokaze.biosci.ohio-state.edu/~dcp/
wimbledon/womble.html
Wimbledon
http://www.city.ac.uk/~sh393/prem/
wimbeldon.htm
Wimbledon
http://www.netkonect.co.uk/b/brenford/
wimbledon/
Wimbledon [unofficial - WISA]
http://www.soi.city.ac.uk/homes/ec564/
donswisa.html
Wimbledon [John's Wimbledon FC page]
http://www.soi.city.ac.uk/homes/ec564/
dons.top.html
Wimbledon (Official)
http://www.wimbledon-fc.co.uk/

ENGLISH DIVISION 1

Birmingham City [PlanetBlues]
http://www.isfa.com/server/web/planetblues/
Birmingham City [BCFC Supports Club
Redditch Branch]
http://www.fortunecity.com/olympia/ovett/
135/
Birmingham City [Richy's B'ham City Page]
http://www.rshill.demon.co.uk/blues.htm
Bradford City
http://www.legend.co.uk/citygent/index.
html
Bury
http://www.brad.ac.uk/%7edjmartin/bury1.
html

Crystal Palace
http://www.gold.net/users/az21/cp_home.
htm
Fulham [The Independent Fulham Fans
Website: History]
http://www.fulhamfc.co.uk/History/history.
html
Fulham [FulhamWeb]
http://www.btinternet.com/~aredfern/
Fulham [Black & White Pages]
http://www.wilf.demon.co.uk/fulhamfc/ffc.
html
Fulham [unofficial - The Fulham Football
Club Mailing List]
http://www.users.dircon.co.uk/~troyj/
fulham/
Fulham
http://zeus.bris.ac.uk/~chmsl/fulham/
fulham.html
Fulham
http://www.netlondon.com/cgi-local/
wilma/spo.873399737.html
Fulham (Official) [mostly merchandising]
http://www.fulham-fc.co.uk
Huddersfield Town
http://www.geocities.com/Colosseum/4401/
index.html
Huddersfield Town
http://ftp.csd.uwm.edu/People/dyce/htfc/
Huddersfield Town
http://granby.nott.ac.uk/~ppykara/htfc/
Huddersfield Town
http://www.uwm.edu:80/~dyce/htfc/index.
html
Ipswich Town [MATCHfacts - Datafile]
http://www.matchfacts.com/mfdclub/
ipswich.html
Ipswich Town
http://www.sys.uea.ac.uk/Recreation/Sport/
itfc/
Ipswich Town [Those Were The Days]
http://www.twtd.co.uk/
Ipswich Town
http://members.wbs.net/homepages/a/d/a/
adamcable.html
Ipswich Town [The Online Portman Vista]
http://www.btinternet.com/~bluearmy/
index2.html
Ipswich Town [unofficial - Latest News -
not really]
http://www.rangey.demon.co.uk/ipswich.htm
Ipswich Town [IPSWICH TOWN tribute]
http://www.geocities.com/Colosseum/Track/
5399/
Ipswich Town [The Ipswich Town VRML Site
- techy, not much else]
http://www.sys.uea.ac.uk/Recreation/Sport/
itfc/vrml/vrml.html
Ipswich Town
http://homepages.enterprise.net/meo/itfc2.
html
Ipswich Town (Official)
http://www.itfc.co.uk/
Manchester City
http://www.uit.no/mancity/
Manchester City (Official)
http://www.mcfc.co.uk/
Middlesbrough
http://www.hk.super.net/~tlloyd/personal/
boro.html
Norwich City
http://ncfc.netcom.co.uk/ncfc/
Oxford United
http://www.aligrafix.co.uk/ag/fun/home/

OxTales/default.html
Oxford United
http://www.netlink.co.uk/users/oufc1/
index.html
Port Vale
http://www.netcentral.co.uk/~iglover/index.
html
Port Vale
http://web.dcs.hull.ac.uk/people/pjp/
PortVale/PortVale.html
Portsmouth [unofficial - History]
http://www.mech.port.ac.uk/StaffP/pb/
history.html
Portsmouth [Links page]
http://www.imsport.co.uk/imsport/ims/tt/
035/club.html
Queens Park Rangers
http://www-
dept.cs.ucl.ac.uk/students/M.Pemble/index.
html
Reading
http://www.i-way.co.uk/~readingfc/
Sheffield United
http://www.shef.ac.uk/city/blades/
Sheffield United
http://pine.shu.ac.uk/~cmssa/bifa.html
Sheffield United (Official)
http://www.sufc.co.uk/
Stoke City
http://www.cs.bham.ac.uk/~jdr/scfc/scfc.
htm
Sunderland (Official)
http://www.sunderland-afc.com/
Swindon Town
http://www.bath.ac.uk/~ee3cmk/swindon/
home.html
Tranmere Rovers
http://www.connect.org.uk/merseyworld/
tarantula/
Tranmere Rovers
http://www.brad.ac.uk/~mjhesp/tran.htm
West Bromwich Albion
http://pages.prodigy.com/FL/baggie/
West Bromwich Albion
http://www.gold.net/users/cp78/
West Bromwich Albion - Official
http://www.wba.co.uk/
Wolverhampton Wanderers [The Wandering
Wolf]
http://www.angelfire.com/wv/Quants/index.
html
Wolverhampton Wanderers
http://www.lazy-dog.demon.co.uk/wolves/
Wolverhampton Wanderers (Official)
http://www.idiscover.co.uk/wolves/

ENGLISH DIVISION 2

AFC Bournemouth
http://www.bath.ac.uk/~ee6dlah/club.htm
AFC Bournemouth
http://www.homeusers.prestel.co.uk/rose220
/afcb1.htm
AFC Bournemouth
http://www.maths.soton.ac.uk/rpb/AFCB.
html
AFC Bournemouth
http://www.maths.soton.ac.uk/rpb/AFCB.
html
AFC Bournemouth
http://www.geocities.com/TimesSquare/
Arcade/7499/afcb.htm
AFC Bournemouth (Official)
http://www.afcb.co.uk/

Blackpool
http://web.ukonline.co.uk/Members/
c.moffat/basil/
Bristol City
http://ourworld.compuserve.com/homepages
/redrobins/
Bristol Rovers
http://dialspace.dial.pipex.co/town/street
/xko88/
Bristol Rovers
http://members.wbs.net/homepages/l/a/r/
lardon/
Bristol Rovers
http://www.cf.ac.uk/uwcc/engin/brittonr/
rovers/index.html
Bristol Rovers
http://www.geocities.com/Colosseum/6542/
Bristol Rovers
http://www.personal.unet.com/~coley/
rovers/
Bristol Rovers
http://www.btinternet.com/~uk/BRFC/
Bristol Rovers
http://www.btinternet.com/~uk/
BristolRovers/index.html
Bristol Rovers
http://www.cowan.edu.au/~gprewett/gas.
htm
Bristol Rovers
http://www.cf.ac.uk/uwcc/engin/brittonr/
rovers/index.html
Burnley
http://www.zensys.co.uk/home/page/trevor.
ent/
Burnley
http://www.theturf.demon.co.uk/burnley.
htm
Burnley
http://www.zen.co.uk/home/page/p.bassek/
Burnley
http://www.mtattersall.demon.co.uk/index.
html
Burnley
http://home.sol.no/~parald/burnley/
Burnley
http://www.geocities.com/Colosseum/7075/
index.html
Carlisle United
http://www.aston.ac.uk/~jonespm/
Carlisle United
http://dspace.dial.pipex.com/town/square/
ad969/
Chester City [Silly Sausage - good history]
http://www.sillysausage.demon.co.uk/
history.html
Chester City (Official)
http://www.chester-city.co.uk/
Gillingham
http://ourworld.compuserve.com/homepages
/gillsf.c/
Grimsby Town
http://www.aston.ac.uk/~etherina/index.
html
Preston North End [unofficial - PNEWeb
HomePage]
http://freespace.virgin.net/paul.billington
/PNEWeb_homepage.html
Preston North End [unofficial - PNE Pages]
http://www.dpne.demon.co.uk/pages/
pagesf.html
Preston North End [pie muncher online -
front door]
http://www.pylonvu.demon.co.uk/pm/pm.
html

BOOKMARKS

Swansea City
http://www2.prestel.co.uk/gmartin/index.
   html
Wrexham
http://www.aber.ac.uk/~deg/wxm/text.html
Wrexham
http://www.csm.uwe.ac.uk/~klhender/wxm/
   index.html
Wycombe Wanderers
http://ourworld.compuserve.com/homepages
   /chairboys/

ENGLISH DIVISION 3

Brighton and Hove Albion
http://www.bmharding.demon.co.uk/
   seagulls/index.html/
Brighton and Hove Albion
http://homepages.enterprise.net/gjc/
Brighton and Hove Albion
http://www.aber.ac.uk/~bmh1/seagulls/
Cardiff City (Official)
http://www.styrotech.co.uk/ccafc/
Cardiff City
http://www.cf.ac.uk/uwcm/mg/bloo/biz.
   html
Cardiff City
http://www.geocities.com/Colosseum/1943/
Cardiff City
http://ds.dial.pipex.com/m4morris/ccafc.
   htm
Chester City
http://www.sillysausage.demon.co.uk/others
   .htm
Halifax Town
http://www.geocities.com/Colosseum/
   Stadium/3043/
Halifax Town [Aussie Style]
http://expage.com/page/Shaymen
Halifax Town [Shaymen]
http://www.shaymen.clara.net/shaymen.html
Hull City
http://www.demon.co.uk/Vox/hullcity/
   hullcity.html
Hull City
http://www.hullcity.demon.co.uk/
Leyton Orient (Official -OriNet)

http://www.matchroom.com/orient/
Leyton Orient [WebOrient - Global Orient
   Website]
http://www.web-orient.clara.net/
Macclesfield Town
http://www.cs.man.ac.uk/~griffitm/
   macctown/
Mansfield Town
http://www.footballnews.co.uk/clubs/1068/
   home.htm
Notts County
http://home.sol.no/~benn/magpienet/
Notts County
http://www.nbs.ntu.ac.uk/Staff/baylidj/
   ncfc.htm
Notts County
http://www.nbs.ntu.ac.uk/Staff/baylidj/
   ncfc.htm
Notts County
http://www.athene.net/soccercity/europe/e
   ng/nc.htm
Notts County
http://www.imsport.co.uk/imsport/ims/tt/
   032/032.html
Scunthorpe United [The Iron Network]
http://www.fortunecity.com/wembley/villa/
   56/index.html
Scunthorpe United [Mailing List]
http://www.isfa.com/isfa/lists/scunthorpe/
Scunthorpe United [Iron World]
http://freespace.virgin.net/su.fc/
Shrewsbury Town
http://www.netlink.co.uk/users/ian/shrews/
   shrews.html
Shrewsbury Town
http://www.shrewsburytown.co.uk/
Swansea City
http://homepages.enterprise.net/gmartin/
Swansea City
http://homepages.enterprise.net/gmartin/
   indexnf.html

SCOTTISH PREMIER LEAGUE

Aberdeen - Official
http://www.afc.co.uk/site/

Aberdeen
http://homepages.enterprise.net/howburn/
Aberdeen
http://www.web13.co.uk/dons/
Aberdeen
http://www.raik.grid9.net/dons/
Aberdeen
http://www.raik.demon.co.uk/dons/
Aberdeen
http://freespace.virgin.net/a.morrison/ajm/
   afchome2.htm
Celtic (Official)
http://www.celticfc.co.uk/presecurity2.html
Celtic
http://www.erols.com/gbrown/dccelts.htm
Celtic
http://www.presence.co.uk/soccer/pages/
   history.html
Dundee United
http://www.algonet.se/~snoe/dfc/
Dundee United
http://www.arabland.demon.co.uk/news.htm
Dunfermline Athletic
http://www.webadvertising.co.uk/wwwboard
   /pars2/
Dunfermline Athletic [Soccernet]
http://www.soccernet.com/scottish/dafc/
   index.html
Dunfermline Athletic
http://www.aiai.ed.ac.uk/~wth/dunfermline/
   dunfermline.html
Heart of Midlothian (Official)
http://www.heartsfc.co.uk/
Heart of Midlothian [No Idle Talk - okay]
http://web.ukonline.co.uk/Members/grant.
   thorburn/nit1.htm
Heart of Midlothian
http://jambos.aurdev.com/update.html
Heart of Midlothian [has a squad list. USA]
http://www.geocities.com/Colosseum/Arena/
   2659/
Heart of Midlothian [Electronic Jam Tart]
http://www.ednet.co.uk/~ricw/
Heart of Midlothian [M'chester Hearts fans]
http://www.rigor.demon.co.uk/manheart.htm
Heart of Midlothian [OrwellHeartsSC]
http://members.aol.com/orwellhsc/

orwellhearts/index.html
Heart of Midlothian [Midlands Hearts]
http://members.aol.com/gsha27/
   midlandhearts1.htm
Heart of Midlothian [Hearts Supporters USA
   - not very informative]
http://jambos.aurdev.com/
Heart of Midlothian [Always The Bridesmaid]
http://ourworld.compuserve.com/homepages
   /a_macdougall_and_ATB/
Heart of Midlothian [Rainbow Hearts S.C.
   Homepage]
http://ourworld.compuserve.com/homepages
   /andy_rainbow_hearts/
Kilmarnock
http://homepages.enterprise.net/wallace/
Kilmarnock
http://www.enterprise.net/kilmarnockfc/
   index.htm
Motherwell
http://www.isfa.com/server/web/
   motherwell/
Rangers (Official) [you need to register]
http://www.rangers.co.uk/channels/
Rangers
http://www.ukfootballpages.com/rangers/
Rangers
http://www.cee.hw.ac.uk/~johnc/Rangers/
   homepage.html
Rangers
http://www.geocities.com/Tokyo/Flats/
   5554/home.html
Rangers
http://www.geocities.com/Colosseum/Field/
   2968/
Rangers
http://dspace.dial.pipex.com/x-static/
   rangers.htm
Rangers
http://www.sgwoozy.force9.co.uk/rangers.
   html
Rangers
http://www.geocities.com/Colosseum/Track/
   7990/
Rangers
http://members.aol.com/broxinet/index.
   html

WEBSITE NOTES

WIN A FREE FOOTBALL BOOK!

Thank-you for buying a copy of our soccer yearbooks, covering all teams in the English Premiership, Scottish Premiership, and English Divisions 1, 2 and 3. We hope that you are happy with your purchase.

This unique collection of yearbooks, gives each supporter in the land their own club diary, supported by all-action shots from the greatest highlights of the last season, plus a diary from July 1998 – June 1999, detailing all club fixtures for the season.

If you would like to be kept informed of other football titles and next season's yearbooks, please cut out and complete this form and mail it back to me: Sharon Pitcher – Marketing Manager, Parragon, 13 Whiteladies Road, Bristol, BS8 1PB. Ten Lucky respondents will receive a free football book for their trouble!

Name of Favourite Team(s) ..Dunfermline..Athletic..
....

Name of Local Team(s) ..Dunfermline..Athletic..
....

Where did you buy this book? ....

Your Name: ..Hannah..Richards..

Street: ..10...Keith..Place...........

Town: ....Dunfermline.................

County: ..Fife...........................

Postcode: ..Ky12...7SR..................

Email: ....

❏ Yes – please keep me informed of other football titles, plus next season's football yearbooks.
This information is being collected on behalf of Parragon Book Services Ltd.

For office use only